NAPLAN
Skills* Handbook

This is not an officially endorsed publication of the NAPLAN program and is produced by Amba Press independently of Australian governments

YEAR 9 TESTS PREPARATION GUIDE

9

Published in 2025 by Amba Press, Melbourne, Australia
www.ambapress.com.au

© Kilbaha Education 2025

This is not an officially endorsed publication of the NAPLAN program and is produced by Amba Press independently of Australian governments.

All rights reserved. No part of this book may be reproduced or transmitted in any form or by any means, electronic or mechanical, including photocopying, recording or by any information storage and retrieval system, without prior permission in writing from the publisher.

Cover design: Tess McCabe
Editor: Rica Dearman

ISBN: 9781923215962 (pbk)
ISBN: 9781923215979 (ebk)

A catalogue record for this book is available from the National Library of Australia.

Contents

Introduction	1
What to expect	3
Revising for NAPLAN	5
Using this book	7
Test days tips	9
Writing test	11
Reading test	17
Language conventions test	46
Numeracy non-calculator test	58
Numeracy calculator test	68
Answers	79

Introduction

What is NAPLAN?

NAPLAN (National Assessment Program – Literacy and Numeracy) is a national test that all Australian students in Years 3, 5, 7 and 9 take each year. Think of it as a way to check how well you're doing with important skills like writing, reading and maths.

What is the purpose of NAPLAN?

NAPLAN helps you, your parents and your teachers understand how you're progressing with these essential skills. It's like a checkpoint to make sure you're on track with your learning and to identify any areas where you might need extra support.

What is being assessed?

NAPLAN tests four main areas:
- Writing (either a narrative or persuasive piece)
- Reading comprehension
- Language conventions (spelling, grammar and punctuation)
- Numeracy (maths and problem-solving)

How is it graded?

Your answers are marked either electronically (for multiple choice) or by trained markers (for writing and text entries). The tests are designed to adjust to your level – if you do well, you'll get harder questions; if you find them tricky, you'll get questions better matched to your level.

What results are provided?

You'll get a detailed report showing how you performed in each area. It shows your individual achievement and how you compare to other students in your year level across Australia.

Why is NAPLAN important?

NAPLAN is important for schools, the government and education planning, but for you personally, it's just one test on one day – it won't affect your grades, high school graduation or future opportunities, so try your best, but don't stress too much about it.

What to expect?

What tests are involved?

You'll complete four different tests:
- Writing
- Reading
- Language conventions
- Numeracy (with both calculator and non-calculator sections)

Why is NAPLAN online?

The online format makes the tests more personalised to your ability level. It's also faster to get results and includes helpful features like being able to flag questions to review later.

When, what and how?

- Tests happen at school in March
- You'll use a computer or tablet
- Each test has a different time limit
- You can use tools like calculators (in certain sections), rulers and protractors when needed
- You can flag questions to come back to later

How does the timer work in NAPLAN online?

The test screen shows a timer that counts down how much time is left. You can choose to hide or show this timer during most of the test, but in the last five minutes, the timer will automatically appear to let you know time is nearly up.

How do audio parts of the test work?

You'll need headphones for some parts of the test, especially for spelling questions and maths problems. The test includes audio that reads out the writing task and maths questions to help you understand them better.

Revising for NAPLAN

Why revise for NAPLAN?

Practising helps you feel more confident and comfortable with the test format. When you're familiar with the types of questions, you can focus on showing what you know rather than worrying about how the test works.

How to revise?

There are many ways to revise. Try some of these:

- Practise similar questions
- Get familiar with the online format using the public demonstration site
- Review topics you find challenging
- Try different question types
- Practise managing your time
- Conduct trial tests

Why do trial tests?

Trial tests help you:

- Get used to the test format
- Practise time management
- Identify areas where you might need more practice
- Feel more confident on test day

Do the tests in this book match those in NAPLAN online?

The questions are similar in style and difficulty to what you'll see in NAPLAN, but remember that the actual online test will adjust to your performance level as you go.

Using this book

How is this book organised?

Each section focuses on one test area (writing, reading, language or numeracy) and includes:

- Practise questions
- Example answers
- Tips and strategies
- Explanations of different question types

Each student in Australia takes the NAPLAN tests in the same order:

Day 1: Writing

Day 2: Reading

Day 3: Conventions of language (grammar, punctuation, spelling)

Day 4: Numeracy

Session 1: Non-calculator

Session 2: Calculator-allowed

How should you use this book?

There are many ways you can use it:

- Start with areas you find most challenging
- Complete the practice tests under timed conditions
- Review your answers and understand any mistakes
- Use the online practice tests to get familiar with the computer format
- Take breaks between practice sessions
- Keep track of topics you need to review more

Practice makes Progress

Test days tips

How to prepare for test days?

Here are some other ways you can prepare for the NAPLAN tests:
- Get a good sleep the night before
- Have a healthy breakfast
- Arrive at school on time
- Bring your water bottle
- Make sure you have the equipment you need (like headphones)
- Download and install the NAPLAN Locked Down browser
- Go to the toilet before the test starts
- Take some slow, deep breaths to stay calm

What happens if you are sick on one of the test days?

Don't worry! If you're sick on test day, stay home and get better. Your school will arrange for you to do the test on another day during the NAPLAN test window. There are catch-up tests available for students who are absent during the main testing period.

What happens if you don't feel you did well on the day?

Remember that NAPLAN is just one test on one day – it's not a pass or fail test. Everyone has good days and bad days. Your teachers look at lots of different ways to assess how you're going at school, not just NAPLAN. If you're worried about your performance, talk to your parents or teachers about it. They can help explain your results when they arrive and provide support if needed.

Stressed? Nervous? Anxious?

Here are some techniques you could use if you feel stressed or nervous during the actual test:

- Take slow, deep breaths – breathe in for four counts, hold for four, breathe out for four
- Remember you can flag difficult questions and come back to them later
- Have a quick stretch in your chair
- Take a sip of water
- Close your eyes for a moment if you need to
- Focus on one question at a time rather than thinking about the whole test
- Remind yourself that you've prepared well and are doing your best
- Use positive self-talk like *I can do this* or *I'll try my best*

Writing test

You have 60 minutes to complete the writing test.

You will be provided with a 'writing stimulus' or 'prompt' – an idea or topic – and asked to write a response of a particular text type (genre).

In the actual NAPLAN test you will write a narrative OR a persuasive piece of writing.

We have provided one test example of each style and some suggestions to keep in mind for each one.

You are to type your answer online but can prepare or plan your response with a pen/pencil and paper.

Marking criteria

Based on the marking guides, here are the 10 criteria you will be assessed on for both persuasive and narrative writing:

1. Audience – the writer's capacity to orient, engage and affect the reader
2. Text structure – the organisation of structural components into an effective text structure
    - For narrative: orientation, complication and resolution
    - For persuasive: introduction, body and conclusion
3. Ideas – the creation, selection and crafting of ideas
4. Content focus
    - For narrative: character and setting (development of character and sense of place/time)
    - For persuasive: persuasive devices (use of devices to enhance the writer's position)
5. Vocabulary – the range and precision of language choices
6. Cohesion – the control of multiple threads and relationships across the text using referring words, substitutions, word associations and text connectives
7. Paragraphing – the segmenting of text into paragraphs that assists the reader
8. Sentence structure – the production of grammatically correct, structurally sound and meaningful sentences
9. Punctuation – the use of correct and appropriate punctuation to aid reading of the text
10. Spelling – the accuracy of spelling and the difficulty of the words used

Writing a strong narrative piece

Your narrative writing will be assessed across 10 key areas. Here is what examiners are looking for:

Structure and organisation

- Start with a clear orientation that sets up your characters and situation
- Develop a complication or problem that creates tension
- Build to an effective resolution that wraps up the story
- Don't just end with 'it was all a dream' or 'they lived happily ever after'
- Use paragraphs to organise different parts of your story

Creating engaging characters and settings

- Bring characters to life through their actions, thoughts, feelings and dialogue
- Show rather than tell: instead of 'She was sad', write 'Tears rolled down her cheeks as she turned away'
- Create atmosphere through descriptive details about the setting
- Help readers visualise the scene through specific sensory details
- Develop the relationship between characters

Vocabulary and language

- Choose precise words that create vivid images: 'prowled' instead of 'walked'
- Use figurative language like similes and metaphors thoughtfully
- Include dialogue that sounds natural and reveals character
- Vary your word choices to maintain reader interest

The River

Today you are going to write a story.

The title for your story is 'The River'.

Your story might be about any adventure, crossing a river or travelling on a river.

It could be about a place close to a river where something important happens.

Your story could be about people who live near a river. They may be helped by the river or put in danger by it.

Think about:

- The characters and where they are
- The complications or problems to be solved
- How the story will end

Remember to:

- Plan your story before you start
- Write in sentences
- Pay attention to the words you choose, your spelling and punctuation
- Check and edit your story when you have finished

Writing a strong persuasive piece

Your persuasive writing will be assessed across 10 key areas. Here is what examiners are looking for:

Vocabulary and spelling

Choose your words carefully to show sophisticated expression. Include:

- Precise words that strengthen your argument (for example, 'essential', 'beneficial', 'crucial')
- Challenging words used correctly (for example, 'environment', 'consequently', 'responsibility')
- Difficult words that demonstrate range (for example, 'evaluate', 'significant', 'analyse')
- Remember: it's better to spell simpler words correctly than to attempt challenging words incorrectly

Sentence structure

Vary your sentences to create impact:

- Use simple sentences for emphasis: 'Animals deserve better'
- Create complex sentences to show relationships between ideas: 'Although some people argue that zoos protect animals, the restricted environment damages their wellbeing'
- Avoid run-on sentences: Instead of 'Animals need space they need freedom they need care', write 'Animals need space, freedom and proper care'
- Watch for comma splices: Instead of 'Zoos can be cruel, they restrict animal movement', write 'Zoos can be cruel because they restrict animal movement'

Every student should play a sport

Do you agree?

Do you disagree?

Perhaps you can think of ideas for both sides.

Write to convince a reader of your opinion.

- **Start with an introduction.** An introduction lets a reader know what you are going to write about.
- **Write your opinion on the topic.** Give reasons for your opinion. Explain your reasons.
- **Finish with a conclusion.** A conclusion sums up your reasons so that a reader is convinced of your opinion.

Remember to:

- Plan your writing
- Use paragraphs to organise your ideas
- Write in sentences
- Choose your words carefully to convince a reader of your opinion
- Pay attention to your spelling and punctuation
- Check and edit your writing so that it is clear for a reader

Reading test

This is a reading test.

There are 46 questions.

You have 65 minutes to complete the reading test.

In this test you will need to read each text, then read each question and choose the correct answer.

Read *Should we abolish zoos?* and then answer questions 1 to 7.

Should we abolish zoos?

JaneyB   **6.21 pm**

We should definitely abolish zoos. It's not fair to keep animals in such small spaces that are nothing like their real habitats. This is especially true for marine animals that don't have enough water to swim around in. The cages at the zoo are really restrictive and confined.

Spaceman   **6.32 pm**

The zoos of today are nothing like the zoos of old. Especially in countries like Australia. There are many very good zoos that have created natural surroundings for their animals, with plenty of foliage to take shelter and space to roam around.

Big Brother   **6.40 pm**

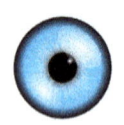

Zoos play a really important part in the survival of endangered species. There are many animals whose natural habitats are being destroyed and are in danger of becoming extinct. Having zoos where these species can be kept alive and where research can be carried out to help them survive is vital.

Johnno   6.43 pm

Zoos are heavily regulated by laws that prohibit any cruelty to animals. Plus they are a great educational resource for people.

JaneyB   6.48 pm

The best way to learn about animals is to observe them in their own habitat in the wild, not in some manufactured setting that humans have made for them. It gives an artificial impression of the animals' behaviours because they are not in a natural setting.

Spaceman   6.50 pm

Again, most zoos do a great job of creating a realistic environment for the animals they keep. Open-range zoos are particularly good at this. The only difference is that the animals are safer in these zoos than they are in their natural habitats because there are no predators.

Should we abolish zoos? questions 1 to 7.

1. **What is Big Brother's main argument?**
   - ○ animals make an important contribution to education
   - ○ animals are protected by laws on cruelty
   - ○ modern zoos are animal friendly
   - ○ zoos make an important contribution to species preservation

2. **JaneyB refers to zoos as *'some manufactured setting'*. What is the tone of this argument?**
   - ○ joking
   - ○ critical
   - ○ practical
   - ○ approving

3. **What are they all likely to agree on?**
   - ○ modern zoos are different to zoos of old
   - ○ animals should be protected
   - ○ zoos are restricted by laws
   - ○ all animals are better off in the wild

4. **JaneyB argues that zoos give humans an *'artificial impression'*. What she means is that**
   - ○ animals in the wild are better off
   - ○ only humans benefit from the existence of zoos
   - ○ animals do not behave realistically in the zoo
   - ○ animals in the zoo are artificial

5. **In her first comment, what is JaneyB's main concern?**
   - zoos are not educational
   - zoos are not realistic
   - zoos keep animals away from their real homes
   - zoos are environmentally unfriendly

6. **Spaceman argues that the only difference between zoo habitats and wild habitats is that *'there are no predators'*. This means that**
   - zoos only keep animals that aren't predators
   - zoos ensure that the animals can't hurt one another
   - humans can view the animals safely
   - wild habitats are better

7. **What effect might this lack of predators have on the animals?**
   _____
   _____

Read the children's non-fiction book review of *Ned Kelly: Black Snake* by Carole Wilkinson below and then answer questions 8 to 12.

The daring of Ned Kelly – book review
By Sally Murphy

Ned Kelly was only 25 years old when he died. Yet within his short life he came to prominence as a thief, a bank robber and a murderer. In the one hundred and twenty two years since his death, he has been portrayed in books, films and in art. Why has he remained such a prominent figure in Australia's history?

Black Snake: The Daring of Ned Kelly offers insight into the life of the outlaw and the chain of events which led to his hanging. In clear, easy-to-understand language, author Carole Wilkinson recounts Kelly's life from birth to his final moments. She details his criminal activities and his life on the run, his family connections and his friendships, giving the reader a detailed idea of the man and his motives.

Each chapter opens with a fictionalised recount from one of the characters present at the various events in Kelly's life, and the text is supported by archival photographs, press clippings and quotes from correspondence and other documents.

This is not a glorification of a criminal career – it is instead a historical exploration of the man who was Ned Kelly, and an exploration of why he chose to lead the life he did. Wilkinson challenges the reader to make their own decision as to whether Kelly was a villain or a hero, a rebel or simply misunderstood.

Author Carole Wilkinson was born in England and came to Australia as a teenager. Writing about history is her passion. Her other titles include the *Ramose* series, set in Ancient Egypt.

Black Snake: The Daring of Ned Kelly by Carole Wilkinson, Black Dog Books, 2002

Children's non-fiction book review: *Ned Kelly: Black Snake* questions 8 to 12.

8. **In *Ned Kelly: Black Snake*, why might the author have opened each chapter with a *'fictionalised recount'*?**
   - ○ it shows Ned Kelly as the terrible villain he was
   - ○ to tell the *story* of Ned Kelly as well as the *history* of Ned Kelly
   - ○ there was not enough accurate information available
   - ○ it allows the reader to make their own decisions

9. **Which sentence best suggests that *Ned Kelly: Black Snake* reveals more about Ned Kelly than other books about the outlaw?**
   - ○ '*...supported by archival photographs*'
   - ○ '*...offers insight into the life of the outlaw*'
   - ○ '*...recounts Kelly's life from his birth*'
   - ○ '*...quotes from correspondence*'

10. **'*This is not a glorification of a criminal career*' – what does this mean?**

   _____

   _____

11. **The *main* purpose of this review is to**
    - ○ inform the reader about Ned Kelly's history
    - ○ inform the reader about the author, Carole Wilkinson
    - ○ recommend *Ned Kelly: Black Snake* for reading
    - ○ explain that this book is different from other histories of Ned Kelly

12. **This review is**
    - ○ a criticism
    - ○ an argument
    - ○ a comment
    - ○ an analysis

Read *Greetings from Luanda, Angola* and then answer questions 13 to 17.

Greetings from Luanda, Angola

The story so far...

During our sixteen months here we've seen much change in Luanda. There's a greater variety of goods for sale and an election, the first for nearly two decades, has brought some hope. The roads are being widened and resealed, the parks are undergoing landscaping and traffic lights are being installed and maintained. Armies of workers (mainly Chinese) toil in the sun, chiselling cubes of stone to fashion patterned footpaths. New hotels are going up, churches are being restored, clinics built and the once beautiful fort that sits above the city is having a facelift.

Of course the traffic is still horrendous, the national airline is still considered a risky ride, and most of the population still lives in shanties without running water or a reliable electricity supply. The people remain friendly, polite and good-natured, but many are desperately poor.

'Amiga! Amiga!' cries the lady in the street. 'Ananas?' She points to the pineapples carried in a huge basket on her head. I think of the two pineapples I've just bought in the market and am about to walk on. Then I see a tiny child strapped to her back and her round stomach just starting to show a baby bump. I buy a pineapple, take it home and give it to the guard.

Christmas in Luanda is a colourful time and this year there seems to be more trees, decorations and 'things to buy' than there were last year. The powers that be have erected a huge tree placed in front of the President's mother's house and several more along major roads. Large orange-flowered jacarandas add splashes of colour to an otherwise drab-grey cement city.

To be continued...

Greetings from Luanda, Angola questions 13 to 17.

13. **In the first paragraph, Luanda is portrayed as**
    - a desolate landscape
    - a place undergoing development
    - a large, bustling city
    - a drab-grey cement city

14. **Why do you think the third paragraph is written in the form of a story?**
    - so that the writing does not become monotonous
    - to ensure that the reader is concentrating
    - to make the scene more impressive
    - to show the reader how the poverty in Luanda affects the writer

15. *'...this year there seems to be more trees, decorations and "things to buy" than there were last year.'* **What does this suggest?**
    - Christmas is becoming more popular in Luanda
    - the President's mother likes Christmas trees
    - Luanda is becoming more prosperous
    - the writer is beginning to like Luanda

16. *'...an election, the first for nearly two decades, has brought some hope'.* **What might they be hoping for?**
    - o less poverty
    - o to leave Luanda
    - o more Christmas merchandise
    - o more markets

17. **Why does the writer change her mind and buy a pineapple?**
    _____
    _____

Read *After the Drought* by Jackie French and then answer questions 18 to 23.

After the Drought

By Jackie French

I rang my mother at two o'clock to say the baby and I were coming visiting.

'I wouldn't if I were you,' she said. 'Have you seen the sky?'

Of course I'd seen the sky. It was much the same as it had been for the past four years – a high tight blue telling you that, frankly, there was no moisture whatsoever hiding at its edges.

I told her so.

'Look again,' she said.

I looked out the window.

Most of the valley was clear – but the valley to the south was shaded, so dark it was hard to see where the trees ended and the sky began.

The shadow spread up the valley like a wedge-tailed eagle unfolding its wings.

The hail began first, great fists of it, so big it was hard to associate them with rain. They bounced off the roof, off the hard-baked ground, rolled down the hill and rested against the fence like tennis balls abandoned after a game.

Then came the smaller hail; fierce pebbles that bit into the soil and left craters or spat up grains of sand. The drops got smaller, smaller, smaller and softer, so there were great piles around the house – hail drifts, in places ankle-deep.

Then the rain began. It was hard to tell it was rain at first, each drop was so fierce and heavy. The world was grey outside, just pouring from the sky.

It was too dense to see what was happening. Suddenly, there was water underneath the door, a foul-smelling trickle that grew stronger and stronger still, till water was round our ankles, knees...

I piled pillows on the bed and put Edward on top. I tried to stop the gaps under the doors, while Edward's father frantically tried to dig drains around the house, but the soil was too hard to drive a pick into, too hard for any rain to penetrate.

The water fell and rolled down the mountain in a fetid wave into the house, carrying with it all the accumulated debris and manure of the past four years.

Then the rain stopped, as suddenly as it had started. The roaring on the roof died down. We opened the doors to sweep the flood away.

Then the roaring began again, like a rumble in the distance, then louder, louder, louder...

We ran outside.

The valley floor was moving. I thought it was an earthquake, the land shuddering after the shock of rain... but it wasn't.

After the Drought questions 18 to 23.

18. **Who is Edward in the story?**

   _____

19. **The water is described as '*a fetid wave*'. From reading the story, what word could best be used in place of the word *fetid*?**
   - furious
   - slow
   - putrid
   - dripping

20. **Why do you think the sky of the previous four years is described as '*tight*'?**
   - it had not rained
   - the sky was stretched
   - the sky was blue
   - the sky was full of rain

21. **Why does the narrator say '*Of course I'd seen the sky*'?**
   - to add a comic element to the narrative
   - to induce intrigue in the reader
   - to highlight the sky in the narrative
   - to suggest that she had been asked a silly question

22. The valley floor is described as *'moving'*. Was it really moving? Please explain your answer.

   _____

   _____

23. What common writing technique is the writer using when she describes the roaring of the flood as *'louder, louder, louder...'*?

    - ○ alliteration
    - ○ repetition
    - ○ construction
    - ○ tautology

Read *Ancient fossil reveals how the turtle's shell evolved* and answer questions 24 to 29.

Ancient fossil reveals how the turtle's shell evolved

Lewis Smith | 27 November 2008

Article from: *The Australian*

FOSSILISED remains of the most ancient turtle yet discovered are helping scientists to unravel the puzzle of how the animal grew its shell.

Only the underside of the turtle is covered by a fully formed protective shell, giving researchers an invaluable glimpse into how it evolved.

The discovery of *Odontochelys semi-testacea* – 'half-shelled turtle with teeth' – is being hailed as the long-sought missing link between turtles that have full shells and their shell-less ancestors.

Three fossilised specimens dug up near Guanling in the southern Chinese province of Guizhou have been dated at 220 million years old and the species has been identified as the ancestor of all other known turtles.

Fossils from the dig have now enabled researchers to discount the theory that the shell originally formed from bony plates, like those on a crocodile, which expanded and fused together.

An international team has concluded that the rival theory that the shell was created when backbones and ribs spread out and joined up to form a hard bony cover is likely to be correct.

Xiao-chun Wu, a palaeontologist at the Canadian Museum of Nature in Ottawa and a member of the research team, said: "Since the 1800s, there

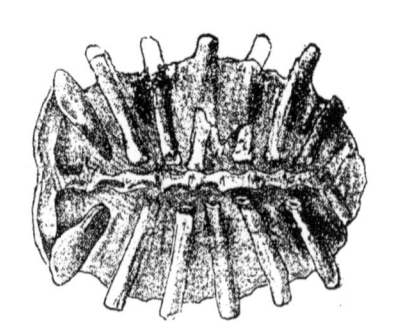

An artist's impression of a ancestral turtle shell from the Triassic Period. AFP

have been many hypotheses about the origin of the turtle shell. Now we have these fossils of the earliest known turtle. They support the theory that the shell would have formed from below as extensions of the backbone and ribs, rather than as bony plates from the skin as others have theorised."

Olivier Rieppel, of the Field Museum in Chicago, added: "This is the first turtle with an incomplete shell. It's difficult to explain how it evolved without an intermediate example."

Because the shell was incomplete the researchers were able to conclude that the shell on the underside of turtles, the plastron, developed before the upper section, the carapace.

The Times

Ancient fossil reveals how the turtle's shell evolved questions 24 to 29.

24. **What is the main discovery discussed in this article?**
    - a half-shelled turtle
    - turtles are more than 220 million years old
    - turtle shells form from bony plates
    - the southern Chinese province of Guizhou

25. **In which period of history did these turtles exist?**
    - Jurassic
    - Guanling
    - Triassic
    - Odontochelys

26. **According to the article, how does this discovery alter the study of turtles?**
    - it proves the theory that turtle shells originate from bony plates
    - it suggests that modern turtles do not need their upper shells
    - it suggests that the upper shells of modern turtles evolved from the ribs
    - it proves that modern turtles do not need their teeth

27. **From reading the text, what word/s could best be used in place of the word '*hypotheses*' (paragraph 6)?**
    - studies
    - theories
    - groups of scientists
    - guesses

28. **The main purpose of this article is to**
    - instruct
    - argue
    - inform
    - hypothesise

29. **The article describes the discovery of these ancient turtles as the '*missing link*' (paragraph 2). This suggests that**
    - scientists now have all the information they need on turtles
    - there were previously no theories on how the turtle shell evolved
    - this presents an entirely new evolutionary theory
    - scientists can now show an evolutionary link between turtles and their shell-less ancestors

Read *Daylight saving time in Australia* and *Daylight saving time overseas* and then answer questions 30 to 35.

DAYLIGHT SAVING TIME IN AUSTRALIA

In Australia, the Federal Government introduced one-hour Daylight Saving Time into all Australian states in 1942. Daylight Saving remained in force until 1944, although Western Australia had already pulled out earlier, on the grounds that it caused inconvenience to workers who followed the sun rather than the clock.

That was the end of Daylight Saving in Australia until 1967, when Tasmania introduced one-hour Daylight Saving Time. Tasmania, the furthest state from the equator at a latitude of 44 degrees, would benefit more from Daylight Saving Time than the mainland states.

In 1971, after much controversy and discussion, one-hour Daylight Saving Time was introduced into New South Wales, Victoria and the Australian Capital Territory. Queensland, much of which is the tropics and which would therefore not get as much benefit from Daylight Saving, reluctantly joined in, but soon abandoned Daylight Saving. In 1974, Western Australia adopted one-hour Daylight Saving Time, but it was thrown out by a referendum in 1975. New South Wales decided to adopt Daylight Saving Time after a referendum in 1976. Even though many of the rural areas were strongly opposed to Daylight Saving, they were out-voted by the more populous city areas.

DAYLIGHT SAVING TIME OVERSEAS

In 1966, the US passed the Uniform Time Act. Within each zone of the US, the Act defined Uniform Daylight Saving Time. Of course, in the Land of The Free, not all of the states followed this recommendation. At first, Daylight Saving Time lasted from the last Sunday in April to the last Sunday in October. The duration of Daylight Saving Time was temporarily extended during 1974 and 1975, thanks to the famous Gasoline Energy Crisis. In 1986, legislation was passed to change this period so it would begin at 2 am on the *first* Sunday in April and cease at 2 am on the last Sunday in October.

Most of the countries of Western Europe have a slightly different schedule – from the last Sunday in March to the last Sunday in September. Britain is different again – from 30 March to 26 October.

Daylight saving time in Australia and *Daylight saving time overseas* questions 30 to 35.

30. **Which Australian state does not appear to have opposed Daylight Savings at any time?**
    o   New South Wales
    o   Queensland
    o   Tasmania
    o   Victoria
    o   Western Australia
    o   Australian Capital Territory

31. **Using your answer from Question 30, why would this state be less opposed to Daylight Saving Time?**

    _____

    _____

32. **What does this article reveal about the practice of Daylight Saving Time?**
    o   it has been the subject of much contention
    o   it is more useful for those states that are closer to the equator
    o   it is always decided upon by referendum
    o   it has been adopted in Australia routinely without argument

33. **Daylight Saving Time in the US currently runs from the**
    o   first Sunday in March to the last Sunday in November
    o   first Sunday in April to the last Sunday in October
    o   last Sunday in March to the last Sunday in September
    o   last Sunday in April to the first Sunday in October

34. In the US, Daylight Saving Time was introduced under *'the Uniform Time Act'*. Why is this an inappropriate name for the Act?

_____

_____

35. The text tells us that Queensland was reluctant to take on Daylight Saving Time because it is tropical and therefore would not benefit as much from Daylight Savings.

    This suggests that

    o the tropics are subject to more temperature fluctuations
    o Queensland is largely a rural state
    o tropical places are closer to the equator
    o its workers follow the sun rather than the clock

Read *A Discovery About My Weird Aunt* and then answer questions 36 to 40.

A Discovery About My Weird Aunt

By Rosemary Nicolls

We had to visit my aunt for the usual Easter egg hunt and family barbecue. A barbecue! (What about the rainforests and methane gas?) She lived a car trip of nearly 200 kilometres away. (Hello, global warming!)

"But she's weird," I said.

"She's my sister," said Mum.

That's sort of what I meant, Mum.

It wasn't even as though she lived near beaches or waterfalls or forests. There was just a house stuck in the middle of paddocks for grazing animals. (More methane gas.) A couple of the grazers were alpacas so at least she didn't use weed killer or a ride-on mower to keep the weedy grass down. Remembering last year's Easter egg hunt, I knew the weirder sister would have nothing to talk about to me.

My brother had been dragged away from the computer – finally, an electro-magnetic-free day for him. His ears were plugged in, though, to a future brain tumour. Mum and Dad had the radio on some sort of Seventies Super Stupid Show, so all I could do was sleep or plug in for half a brain tumour. I chose to dream of a cleaner, greener, cooler environment.

We stopped for a fat and sugar overdose at Nasty Fasty on the way. I hoped my aunt had some green, crunchy stuff to help the digestion.

As we turned off the road, I saw things that hadn't been there before – black rectangles on the roof of her house and a very tall, very thin pole with a whirring, purring blade.

"That's sun and wind power!" I exclaimed.

"Weird," murmured Mum.

My aunt had gone green. We would be able to communicate after all.

A Discovery About My Weird Aunt questions 36 to 40.

36. **What was the narrator's primary worry about the trip to his aunt's house?**

    ○ the animals grazing the paddocks producing methane gas

    ○ his brother being dragged away from the computer

    ○ not being able to relate to his aunt

    ○ having to listen to the Seventies Super Stupid Show

37. **'...a very tall, very thin pole with a whirring, purring blade.' What is the narrator describing?**

    ○ solar power

    ○ a wind turbine

    ○ a ride-on mower

    ○ a flag pole

38. **'I chose to dream of a cleaner, greener, cooler environment.' In this sentence, what is the narrator revealing about himself?**

    ○ he is tired of listening to music

    ○ he is a conservationist

    ○ he does not understand his aunt

    ○ he believes fat and sugar are bad for people

39. **What realisation does the narrator reach?**

    ○ his mother is also a greenie

    ○ his brother does not share his beliefs

    ○ barbeques produce methane gas

    ○ his aunt is sympathetic to his cause

40. **What is one effect of this story being told in the first person?**
    - it gives the impression of distance from the scene
    - it offers deeper insight into the mindset of the narrator
    - it allows the reader to feel compassion toward the other characters
    - it enables the writer to comment with a superior approach

Read *Wellington* and then answer questions 41 to 46.

Wellington

By Aoife Bearsley

Wellington is a small, sea-smacked city on the bottom coast of the North Island of New Zealand. Here, the land folds over itself in wrinkles and bulges and multicoloured, weatherboard houses are pressed up and tucked down into the hills. Letterboxes perched on the curbsides seem homeless as the land falls away from the edges of roads that wind down into roof-dappled valleys of pine and gorse. From those same curb sides, on a clear day, you can see yachts swarming on the bay and the Remutuka Mountains amassed in the north. Or, you might see a fearsome, blackened sky rolling above you as a southerly roars up from the Antarctic.

Because New Zealand lies over one of the Earth's most active fault lines, all the architecture in Wellington is built on moving foundations. Those buildings made with glass, steel and brick are laid squat on the Quay and wood is used wherever possible, because it bows and flexes more readily than concrete and steel. The many timber houses rattle and sway with frequent tremors and the ever-present winds that howl across Cook Strait and into the harbour.

Wellington questions 41 to 46.

41. *'Those buildings made with glass, steel and brick are laid squat on the key.'* **What does this reveal about buildings of this type in Wellington?**

   o   they are laid down gently

   o   they are all flat-roofed

   o   they are not tall high-rises

   o   they all look the same

42. **Why do the letterboxes seem 'homeless'?**

   _____

   _____

43. **What does the phrase *'yachts swarming on the bay'* imply?**

   o   the yachts look like ants

   o   there are many yachts sailing in the bay

   o   the yachts don't know where they are going

   o   the yachts are moored

44. **Wellington is described in the text as a *'sea-smacked'* city. What does this suggest?**

   o   the city's coastal sea can be fierce

   o   the city is an island

   o   the city's buildings are eroding

   o   the city is a naval port

45. **What word below best describes the style of writing used in this piece?**
    - conversational
    - dictatorial
    - satirical
    - descriptive

46. **'Here, the land folds over itself in wrinkles and bulges.' This phrase is**
    - fictional
    - literal
    - metaphorical
    - demonstrative

Language conventions test

This is the language conventions test (which covers spelling, grammar and punctuation).

There are 50 questions.

You have 50 minutes to complete the language conventions test.

There will be a mix of question types including:

- Multiple choice
- Short answer
- Error identification/correction
- Fill in the blank/missing word

The test typically starts with spelling questions before moving into grammar and punctuation. You need to identify errors and show your understanding of correct language usage through these various question formats.

Spelling

The spelling mistakes in these sentences have been circled. Write the correct spelling for each circled word in the box.

1. Humans will need to investigate (renewabbel)

2. sources of energy to (adress)

3. the (enourmitty) of the problems

4. (curantly) faced by the world through global warming.

5. Jack showed his strength when he carried that heavy sack of (potatos) all the way home.

6. Everyone comments on how (musculler)

7. he is, but it was still very (impresive.)

8. He wore a (disgize) that was so

9. effective that not even his own family could (gess) who he was.

**Each sentence has one word that is incorrect.
Write the correct spelling of the word in the box.**

10. I don't want to make a dental apointment.

11. This is the highest temprature ever recorded.

12. Wendy looked glamerous in her new outfit.

13. Hippopotamuses can be very feroshus animals.

14. She studied hard for her quallifications.

15. Thongs are not approprate as formal dress.

16. Bad behaviour should have a consequense.

17. Their going to Europe on a vacation.

18. The detour was a great inconveniance.

19. The car stood motionless in trafic.

20. Enthusiasm is another word for pasion.

21. Jo feels priviledged to reside in Australia.

22. His study habits prepared him for the examanation.

23. The origin of the universe is a mistery.

24. Tran got a sneak preeview of the movie.

25. Mark loves recieving presents on his birthday.

Grammar and punctuation

26. Which of the following correctly completes the sentence?

Tom _____ better, but he did not want to.

would have done	had done	could have done	done
○	○	○	○

27. Which sentence has the correct punctuation?

○ Did he say, "Good morning, Dave"?
○ Did he say "Good morning,Dave"?
○ Did he say good morning Dave?
○ Did he say, "Good morning, Dave?"

28. Which of the following correctly completes the sentence?

I asked, "_____ bag has been left on the floor?"

Whose'	Who's	Whos	Whose
○	○	○	○

29. Which of the following correctly completes the sentence?

She _____ for a long time about her actions before she made that apology.

has thought	had thought	thinks	will think
○	○	○	○

30. Which of the following correctly completes the sentences?

I'm confused. Raffy said that he would be late, _____ he arrived on time.

so	yet	when	if
○	○	○	○

31. Which of the following correctly completes the sentence?

They _____ driven more slowly in the rain.

should of	should'ave	should've	shouldve
○	○	○	○

32. Which sentence has the correct punctuation?

○ Our societys future will rely upon people's willingness to act.

○ Our societies future will rely upon people's willingness to act.

○ Our society's future will rely upon peoples willingness to act.

○ Our society's future will rely upon people's willingness to act.

33. Which of the following correctly completes the sentence?

He drove the car _____ .

extremely quickly	extreme quick	extreme quickly	extremely quick
○	○	○	○

34. Which of the following correctly completes the sentence?

The restaurant had an _____ atmosphere that attracted customers.

vibrant	warm	alluring	joyful
○	○	○	○

35. Shade one bubble to show where the missing question mark (?) should go.

Did you just ask, "Which questions should I do," even though I just told you
↑ ↑ ↑ ↑
○ ○ ○ ○

36. Which sentence has the correct punctuation?

    ○ Taylor plays the piano; but Sam plays the guitar.

    ○ Taylor plays the piano; Sam plays the guitar.

    ○ Taylor plays the piano; and Sam plays the guitar.

    ○ Taylor plays the piano. Sam plays the guitar;

37. Which of the following has the correct punctuation?

    ○ Stephan's mum drove him to school. He doesn't like walking.

    ○ Stephans mum drove him to school. He doesn't like walking.

    ○ Stephan's mum drove him to school. He doesnt like walking.

    ○ Stephan's mum drove him to school he doesn't like walking.

38. Which of the following correctly completes the sentence?

Some people prefer savoury food _____ sweet food.

from	than	to	for
○	○	○	○

39. Which sentence has the correct punctuation?

　○ Bring three things a pen, some paper: and something to eat.

　○ Bring three things a pen, some paper and something to eat.

　○ Bring three things: a pen some paper, and something to eat.

　○ Bring three things: a pen, some paper and something to eat.

40. Which of the following has the correct punctuation?

　○ If you are ill. You should see a doctor.

　○ If you are ill; you should see a doctor.

　○ If you are ill: you should see a doctor.

　○ If you are ill, you should see a doctor.

41. Which sentence has the correct punctuation?

○ Suddenly a large bird swooped down swallowed a bug and flew off.

○ Suddenly, a large bird swooped down, swallowed a bug and flew off.

○ Suddenly a large bird, swooped down, swallowed a bug, and flew off.

○ Suddenly a large bird swooped down, swallowed a bug and, flew off.

42. Which sentence has the correct punctuation?

○ The book, that I borrowed, from you was, excellent.

○ The book, that I borrowed from you, was excellent.

○ The book that I borrowed from you, was excellent.

○ The book that I borrowed from you was excellent.

Grammar

Read *Internet Versus World Wide Web* and then answer questions 43 and 44.

Internet Versus World Wide Web	

The terms 'Internet' and 'World Wide Web' are often used in everyday speech without much distinction. However, they are not the same. The Internet is a global data communications system that allows computers to connect, whereas the Web is just one of the services that the Internet can provide. It links documents and resources through hyperlinks and URLs.

43. The word *Internet* is capitalised because it is

- ◯ a proper noun
- ◯ a common noun
- ◯ an adjective
- ◯ an adverb

44. In the last sentence, the word *links* is used as

- ◯ a proper noun
- ◯ a common noun
- ◯ a verb
- ◯ an adverb

Read *Banjo Paterson* and answer questions 45 to 47.

BANJO PATERSON

'Banjo' Paterson was born Andrew Barton Paterson at Narrambla on 17 February 1864. In 1895, at the age of 31, Paterson achieved two milestones in Australian writing. He composed his famous *Waltzing Matilda* and the classic *The Man from Snowy River*. Paterson's role in Australian culture has been celebrated on the Australian $10 note.

45. This text is written in the

    ◯ past tense

    ◯ present tense

    ◯ future tense

46. In the first sentence, the word *Banjo* is in inverted commas (' ') because

    ◯ it is a strange word

    ◯ it is a nickname

    ◯ it is a word from a foreign language

    ◯ it is a technical word

47. The word *famous* used before *Waltzing Matilda* is used as

    ◯ a proper noun

    ◯ a common noun

    ◯ an adjective

    ◯ an adverb

Read *Expanding Universe* and then answer questions 48 to 50.

EXPANDING UNIVERSE

We now believe that the universe is expanding. The idea is that our universe is expanding like an inflating balloon, and galaxies are getting further apart from one another in the same way that if we were to draw three dots on our balloon, and then inflate it, the dots would get further apart at a consistent rate. Our universe is one big inflating balloon and our galaxies little dots drawn upon it.

48. This text has been written in the

    ○ first person

    ○ second person

    ○ third person

49. '*Our universe is expanding like an inflating balloon*' is an example of

    ○ a simile

    ○ a metaphor

    ○ alliteration

    ○ personification

50. '*Our universe is one big inflating balloon*' is an example of a

    ○ a simile

    ○ a metaphor

    ○ alliteration

    ○ personification

Numeracy non-calculator test

This is a numeracy non-calculator test.

You have 40 minutes to complete the non-calculator test. There are 32 questions in this test.

You cannot use a calculator, but you can use pen and paper to work out things.

This test focuses on basic numerical calculations and mathematical thinking without tools.

Both the numeracy non-calculator and numeracy calculator tests use similar mathematical concepts including:

♦ Number and algebra

♦ Measurement and geometry

♦ Statistics and probability

You will get a break between the two tests on the day, however, they will both be completed on the same day.

1. What is the missing number in the pattern?

   94 88 ? 76

2.

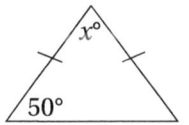

   What is the value of x in the above triangle?

3.

x	-2	-1	0	1	2
y	4	1	0	1	4

   Which one of the following graphs shows the information in the above table?

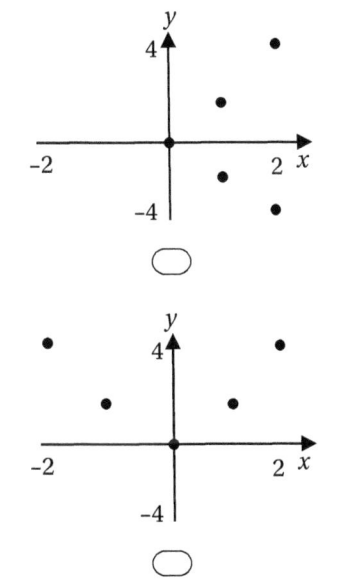

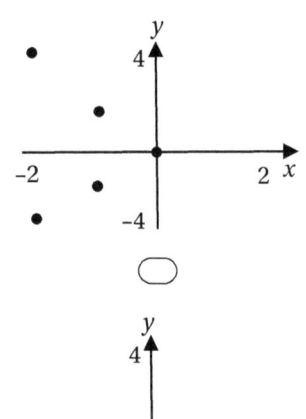

4. The heights of students in Year 9 were recorded in the following stem and leaf:

14	1	3	7	7	9	
15	0	2	2	4	7	8	9
16	0	2	3	5	9	

Key
14/1 = 141 cm

How many students have a height of less than 152 cm?

5	6	7	8
○	○	○	○

5.

A rectangle ABCD with AB = $3x - 10$ and DC = $2x + 7$.

If ABCD is a rectangle, then what is the value of x?

3	5	13	17
○	○	○	○

6. 30 discs coloured green or yellow are placed in a bag so that $\frac{5}{6}$ of the discs are yellow. What is the ratio of green to yellow discs in the bag?

5:6	6:5	1:5	5:1
○	○	○	○

7. A car travels at 120 km/hr. How many metres does it travel in one second?

[   ] m

8. Liam rides 5 km south from his home to school, then 3 km east to the library, then 9 km north to the swimming pool. To return home from the swimming pool which way could he go?

3 km west and 4 km south	3 km west and 5 km south	3 km east and 5 km south	9 km south and 3 km east
○	○	○	○

9. One Australian dollar buys 0.70 American dollars. How many American dollars can Sam buy with 300 Australian dollars?

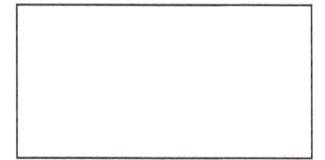

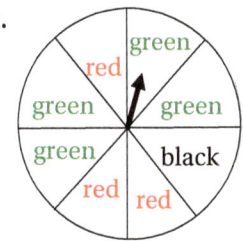

10. If the spinner above is spun once, then what is the chance of it pointing to green?

1:2	3:4	4:3	4:4
○	○	○	○

11. Which one of the following expressions is equivalent to $-5(2 - 3x)$?

$-7 - 8x$	$-7 + 8x$	$-10 + 15x$	$-10 - 15x$
○	○	○	○

12. What is the value of *a*?

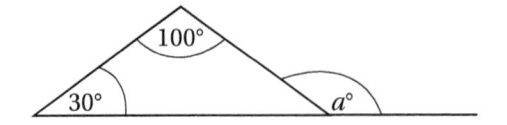

13.

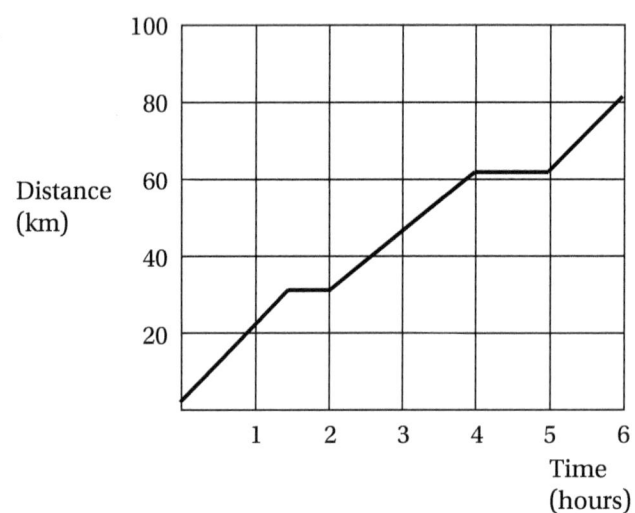

The graph above shows Mike's bike ride. How much of this ride did he spend resting?

$\frac{1}{2}$ hr	1hr	$1\frac{1}{2}$ hrs	5hrs
○	○	○	○

14. What mixed number has the same value as $\frac{33}{22}$?

$1\frac{2}{33}$	$1\frac{3}{22}$	$1\frac{1}{2}$	$2\frac{1}{11}$
○	○	○	○

15.

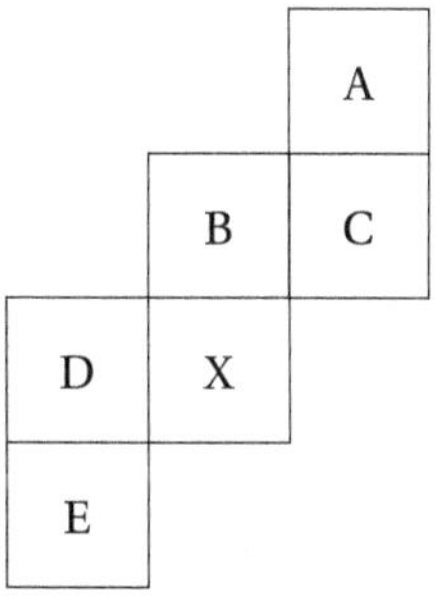

The above net is made into a cube.

What is the name of the face opposite the face named **X**?

A	C	D	E
⬭	⬭	⬭	⬭

16. The reflex angle ABC 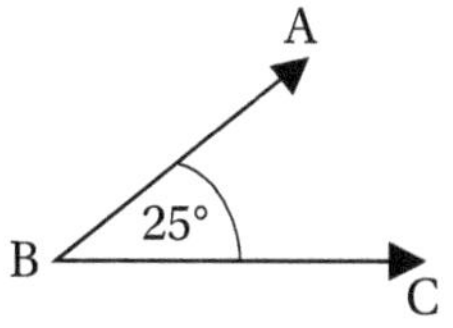 is equal to

145°	155°	335°	345°
⬭	⬭	⬭	⬭

17.

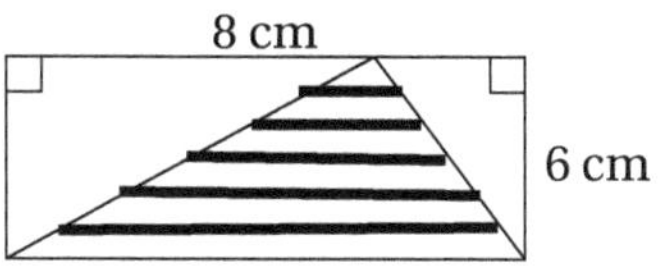

What is the area of the shaded section of the above diagram?

cm^2

18.

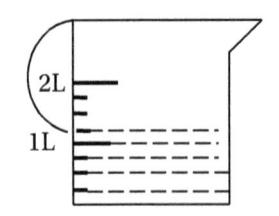

If Lynn adds 35 ml of liquid to the water in the above jug, how many litres of liquid will then be in the jug?

1.6	1.285	1.35	2.35
○	○	○	○

19. What is 0.03 as a percentage?

20. Which ordered pair satisfies the equation $\frac{y}{2} - x = 6$?

(−4, 8)	(0, 6)	(2, 16)	(3, −6)
○	○	○	○

21. What is the answer to 8.4 ÷ 0.4?

22. If $\frac{x}{x-5} = 6$, then what is the value of x?

23. When the above shape is rotated 270° in an anticlockwise direction, then which one of the following will be the image?

24. Jack, Jill, Phil, Poppy and Iris are playing tennis in a round robin. If each person must play a match against every other person, how many matches must be played?

25. The sum of three consecutive numbers is 174. What is the smallest of these consecutive numbers?

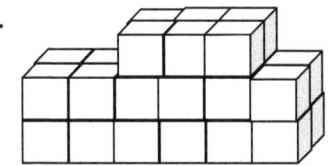

26. The above shape is built using cubes, each with a volume of one cubic centimetre. The whole of the outside is then spraypainted. How many of the cubes would have paint on three sides only?

27. What is the value of $5p^3$ when $p = -2$?

−40	−30	30	40
○	○	○	○

28. Which one of the following is the graph of the line $y = 3x$?

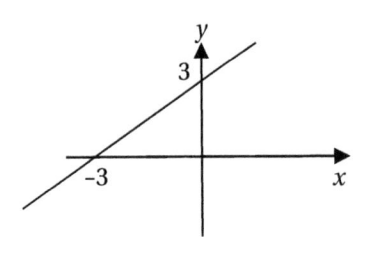

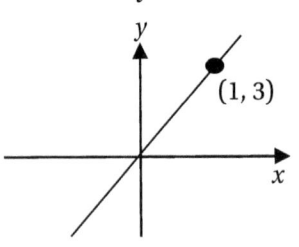

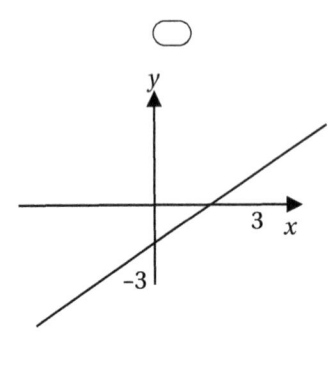

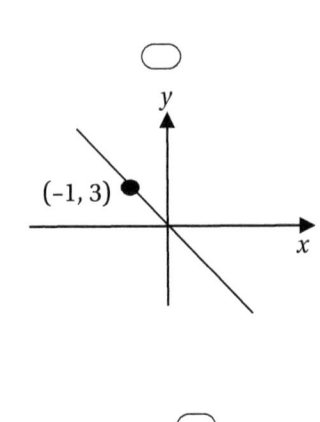

29. How many rectangular boxes 2 cm by 2 cm by 6 cm can fit into a crate 20cm by 20cm by 60cm?

30. A car has a petrol tank with a capacity of 72 L. Bev sets out on a trip with the tank 75% full. If 50% of this petrol is used up, how many litres of petrol must Bev now put in the car to completely fill the tank?

31. A number of children boarded the school bus to go home. At the first stop $\frac{1}{3}$ of the children got off. At the next stop $\frac{1}{4}$ of the remaining children got off. At the next stop $\frac{1}{2}$ of the children still on the bus got off. If there were now 6 children on the bus, how many children got on the bus at the school?

32.

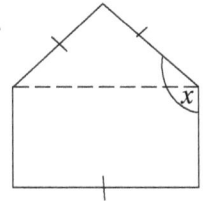

The above pentagon is formed by placing an equilateral triangle on a rectangle as shown.

What is the value of the angle marked x?

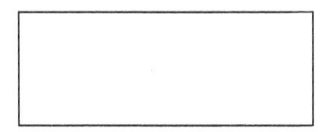

Numeracy calculator test

This is a numeracy calculator test.

You have 40 minutes to complete the numeracy calculator test.

This test has 32 questions to complete.

For your NAPLAN numeracy test, you'll have to use the calculator that's built into the test – you can't bring your own. This online calculator might feel a bit different from what you use in class, so here's a tip: practise using it before test day so you're comfortable with how it works. That way, you won't waste time during the test trying to figure out how it works. Remember, it's just a basic scientific calculator with standard functions, so once you've played around with it a bit, you'll be fine!

This test focuses on basic numerical calculations and mathematical thinking without tools.

Both the numeracy non-calculator and numeracy calculator tests use similar mathematical concepts including:

- Number and algebra
- Measurement and geometry
- Statistics and probability

You will get a break between the two tests on the day, however, they will both be completed on the same day.

1.

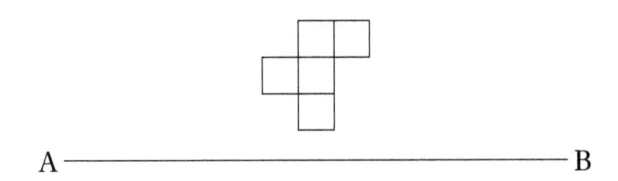

If the above shape is rotated 90° in an anticlockwise direction and then flipped over the line AB, which one of the following shapes would it look like?

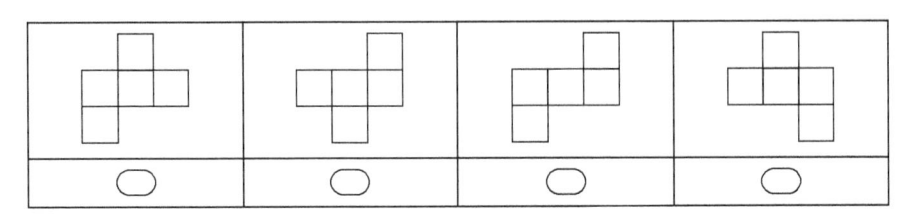

○	○	○	○

2. Which number is exactly halfway between $5\frac{2}{3}$ and $8\frac{1}{3}$?

$6\frac{1}{3}$	$6\frac{2}{3}$	7	$7\frac{1}{3}$
○	○	○	○

3. What is the average (mean) of 11.7, 14.42, 16.84?

13.94	14.14	14.32	14.42
○	○	○	○

4. If $a = 9$, what is the value of $3a$?

12	27	39	81
○	○	○	○

5. Which dotted line is a line of symmetry?

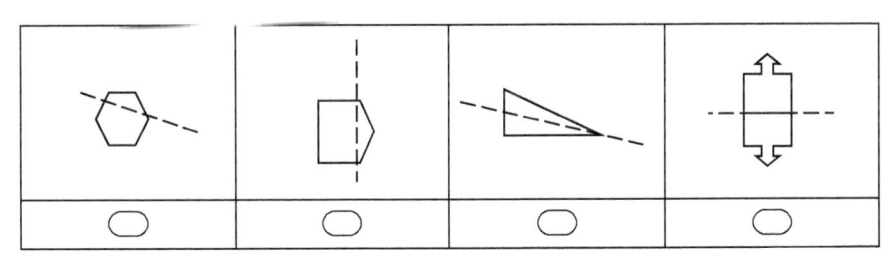

○	○	○	○

6.

Using the graph above, which one of the following statements is true?

○ Beth walked faster than Amy
○ Colin walked faster than Beth
○ Colin walked further than Amy
○ Colin walked faster than both Beth and Amy

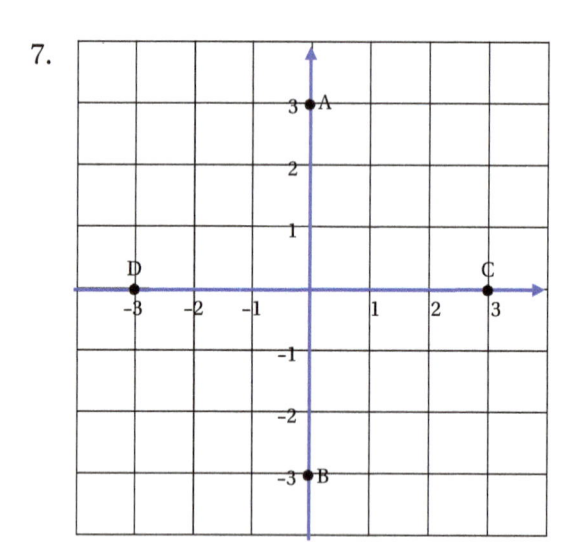

7.

On the coordinate axes above, which point is the point (0,-3)?

A	B	C	D
○	○	○	○

8. The diameter of a circular disc is 1.4 cm. What is the area of this disc to the nearest square centimetre?

2 cm²	4 cm²	6 cm²	9 cm²
○	○	○	○

9. If $p = 4$, what is the value of $\dfrac{10p}{5p - 10}$?

$-\dfrac{1}{5}$	$\dfrac{1}{5}$	4	8
○	○	○	○

10.

x	0	1	2
y	9	4	1

A table of values of x and y is given above. Which one of the following is the correct rule for y in terms of x?

$y = 2x + 1$	$y = 3x^2$	$y = 4x - 1$	$y = (x - 3)^2$
○	○	○	○

11.

If the area of the shaded region in the above diagram is 25 m², what is the area of the unshaded region?

50 m²	100 m²	125 m²	175 m²
○	○	○	○

12. 60% of Year 9 students at a certain school are in the choir. If 156 Year 9 students at this school are *not* in the choir, how many students are in Year 9 at this school?

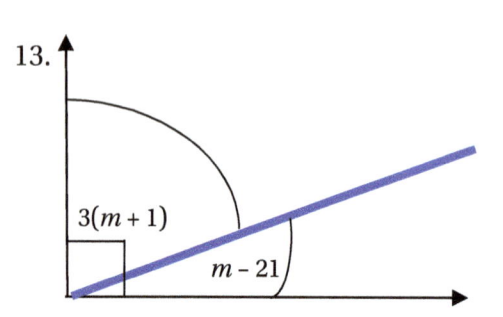

13. What is the value of m in the above diagram?

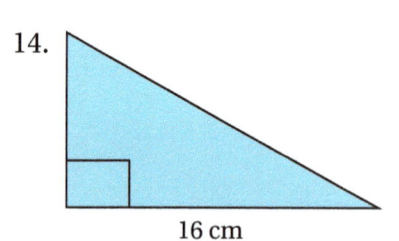

(Diagram shows angle with $3(m+1)$ and $m-21$)

14. The above triangle has an area of 160 cm². If the triangle is reduced in size so that the base is half the original size and the height is half the original size, then what is the area of the reduced triangle?

cm²

15.

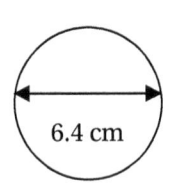

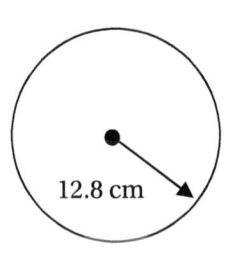

6.4 cm   12.8 cm

What is the ratio of the circumference of the smaller circle to the larger circle?

8:1	1:8	4:1	1:4
○	○	○	○

16. If $y = 25 - 5x$, then what is the value of y when $x = 3.15$?

9.25	9.85	16.85	63
○	○	○	○

17. Peter left home at 4:20 pm on Thursday and arrived at his destination at 7:14 am on the following day.

How long did his journey take?

hours   mins

18. A rectangle has an area of 115 m². If the width of the rectangle is 6.25 m, then what is the length of the rectangle?

m

19.

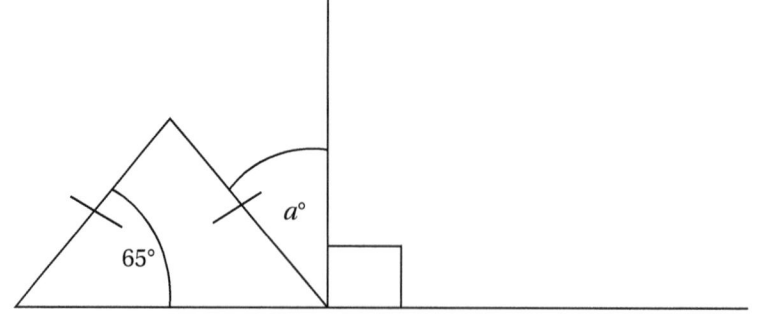

What is the value of a?

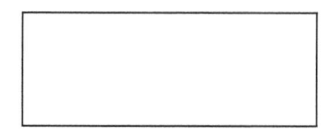

20. Last year Nikita's wage was $280 per week. This year she received a 30% increase and has been told that next year she will get another 20% increase. What will her weekly wage be next year?

$

21. Round 436.2587 to the nearest hundredth.

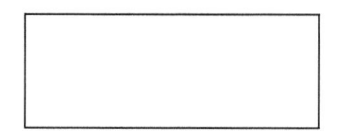

22. 42 Year 6 students at the Learn Well Primary School catch the bus each day. If this is 30% of the Year 6 students, how many students are in Year 6?

23.

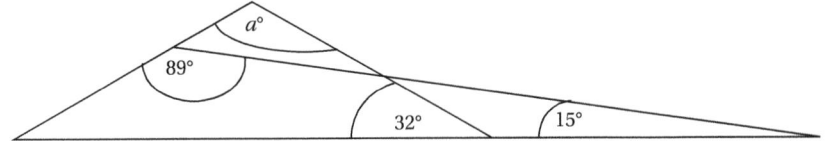

What is the value of *a* in the above diagram? (diagram not to scale)

59°	72°	76°	116°
○	○	○	○

24. Mike has a mobile phone. When he makes 12 calls in a month the cost is $22.20. When he makes 60 calls in a month the cost is $39. Which rule can be used to find the cost of *n* calls?

$16.2 + 0.5n$	$4n - 25.8$	$18 + 0.35n$	$159 - 2n$
○	○	○	○

25. When an object is dropped from a height, the distance, *d* metres, it has fallen at time, *t* seconds, is given by the equation $d = \frac{1}{2} \times 9.8t^2$. How far does the object fall in the first three seconds?

m

26.

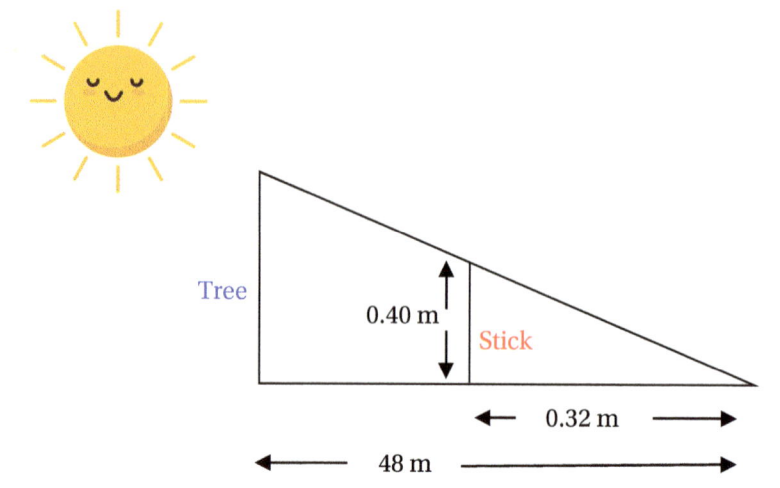

A stick 0.40 m long casts a shadow 0.32 m long. At the same time of day, a tree casts a shadow 48 m long. How high is the tree?

38.4 m	48.08 m	48.72 m	60 m
○	○	○	○

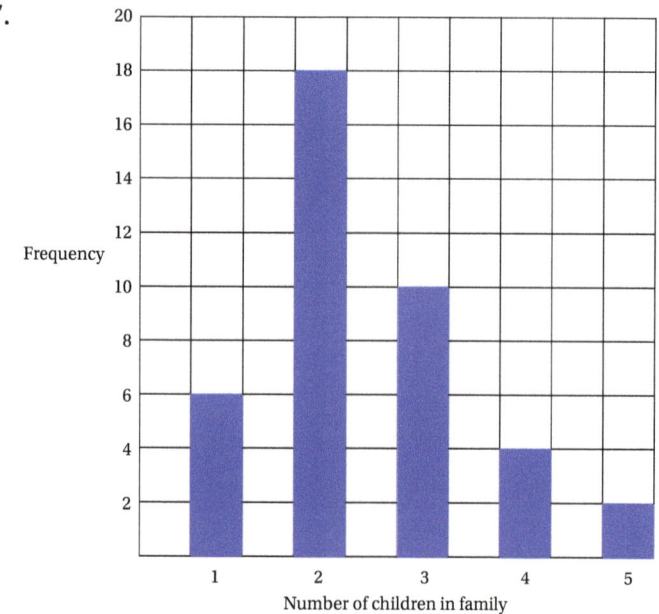

27.

Number of children in family

A number of people were surveyed to see how many children were in each of their families. The graph on the previous page shows the results. How many people were surveyed?

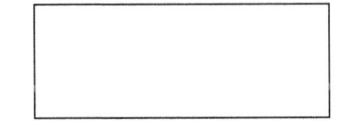

28. The rule, multiply by 5 and then subtract 2, is used to work out the following pattern

    3 , 13 , 63 . . .

    What is the next number in the pattern?

29. A number p is squared and then multiplied by 2, and then 5 is added to this answer.

    Which of the following is the correct algebraic expression?

$2p^2 + 5$	$(2p)^2 + 5$	$2(p^2 + 5)$	$4p^2 + 10$
○	○	○	○

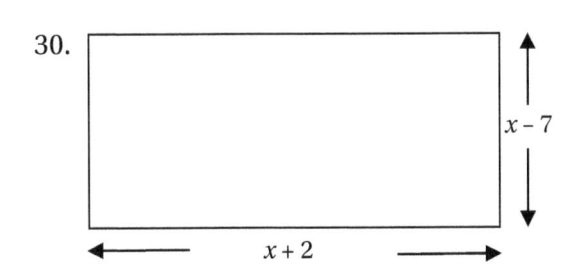

30.

$x - 7$

$x + 2$

What is the area of the above rectangle in terms of x?

$x^2 - 5x - 14$	$x^2 - 5x + 14$	$x^2 + 5x + 14$	$x^2 + 5x - 14$
○	○	○	○

31. Granny Joan shared $245 among her three grandchildren. If the eldest received twice as much as the middle child and the youngest received half as much as the middle child, how much did the youngest child get?

$

32. The mean height of a class of 24 students is 152 cm. A new girl, Suzie, who is 127 cm, joins the class. What is the mean height of the class now?

cm

Answers

Writing sample responses

The River

It was school camp time again. We were going to set up our tents near the banks of the King River. I didn't think it would be a king river at all. I doubted if Melbourne or Victoria would ever have real rain again. You know, the sort that sends you to sleep at night without your earphones. Everyone calls me a greenie but, secretly, I was relieved that the desalination plant was going ahead. Our water certainly wasn't coming down from the skies any more.

At the base we were given our tents, mattresses and other equipment. Strange-looking tops and bottoms with long sleeves and legs were handed out.

"Maybe they're for mosquito protection!"

"They look like jail uniforms!"

"They probably help in the brain-washing for a cult."

Our leader, who remembered the olden days, explained that they were waterproofs, in case of rain. Didn't he know we would never need them?

After literally hours of walking our leader called out, "Nearly there! Just the other side of the river."

River? A gutter with puddles! A boat was mockingly tied to a tree a hundred metres away.

The next few days were fine and sunny. What else would they be? We crossed the gutter-with-puddles twice a day for various activities. On the last morning we were told to put on our walking-through-water gear. Did our leader have in-built weather radar? He had found out something we didn't know.

Amazing! The gutter-with-puddles was a raging torrent.

"Stop exaggerating, Rosie," contradicted the leader. "It's no more than sixty centimetres deep. They've let water down from the weir. We're going to have to use the boat to ferry the packs and the midgets across."

At least we learned how much fun a real river was and I found out another use for the mosquito-repelling cult uniforms. I wore them after being pushed into the water for being chief whinger.

Every student should play a sport

Contrary to the popular Australian belief, I do not support the view that all students should play a sport. In fact, I believe that schools put too much money and time into ensuring that every student actively participates in all types of sport. If schools do not have their own ovals, they have to hire playing fields and pay for buses to take their students to and from these venues. Surely the time and money thus spent could be put to better use in buying resources and teaching the academic subjects that are essential for passing Year 12 and getting into university.

Some students have a real fear of being hurt in certain contact sports that are popular among the school hierarchy, and some students just have a weekly lesson in once again experiencing failure because the school exploits a winning culture. Surely sport cannot be good, psychologically, for such students.

Then there are those parents who want to live their shattered dreams, of being a great sportsperson, through their children and they urge them to win at all costs. At team sporting events, such parents can become hostile and nasty, yelling barbaric insults or even physically abusing any student who gets in the way of their child's success. In individual events, such parents know the times of every competitor and relentlessly urge their offspring to work harder and longer in order to succeed. In order to appease such parents, some children can resort to drugs to give them an advantage over their competitors.

This has the effect of teaching the young players all the negative characteristics that should never be associated with sport. From such parents, the child learns that winning, not playing, is the most important aspect of sport. Such parents emphasise competition, rather than cooperation, cheating rather than fair play and always winning rather than sometimes accepting a loss graciously. These are contrary to the life skills such children will need as adults when they will certainly have to deal with working with others, trading fairly in business and coping when things do not always go their way.

While some children can benefit from playing sport, some children will definitely be hindered in life because of their experiences.

Reading

Should we abolish zoos?

1. **What is Big Brother's main argument?**
   - ○ animals make an important contribution to education
   - ○ animals are protected by laws on cruelty
   - ○ modern zoos are animal friendly
   - ● zoos make an important contribution to species preservation

   Zoos make an important contribution to species preservation is the correct answer. The main focus of Big Brother's argument is that zoos play an important part in the survival of endangered species.

2. **JaneyB refers to zoos as '*some manufactured setting*'. What is the tone of this argument?**
   - ○ joking
   - ● critical
   - ○ practical
   - ○ approving

   Critical is the correct answer. JaneyB is clearly against animals being kept in a manufactured setting.

3. **What are they all likely to agree on?**
   - ○ modern zoos are different to zoos of old
   - ● animals should be protected
   - ○ zoos are restricted by laws
   - ○ all animals are better off in the wild

Animals should be protected is the best answer. All the writers in this forum show, through their arguments, that they each care for animals despite their differing opinions on zoos.

4. **JaneyB argues that zoos give humans an '*artificial impression*'. What she means is that**
   - ○ animals in the wild are better off
   - ○ only humans benefit from the existence of zoos
   - ● animals do not behave realistically in the zoo
   - ○ animals in the zoo are artificial

   Animals do not behave realistically in the zoo is the best answer. Though JaneyB is likely to agree with most of the answers, the question is asking us what JaneyB means when she talks about animals in the zoo giving an 'artificial impression.'

5. **In her first comment, what is JaneyB's main concern?**
   - ○ zoos are not educational
   - ○ zoos are not realistic
   - ● zoos keep animals away from their real homes
   - ○ zoos are environmentally unfriendly

   Zoos keep animals away from their real homes is the correct answer. The question refers specifically to JaneyB's first comment, in which she states that it is 'not fair to keep animals in such small spaces that are nothing like their real homes.'

6. **Spaceman argues the only difference between zoo habitats and wild habitats is that *'there are no predators'*. This means that**
   - ○ zoos only keep animals that aren't predators
   - ● zoos ensure that the animals can't hurt one another
   - ○ humans can view the animals safely
   - ○ wild habitats are better

   ***Zoos ensure that the animals can't hurt one another** is the best answer. A predator is an animal that preys on another. Zoos still have animals that are predators, but they are kept in habitats in which they cannot prey on other animals.*

7. **What effect might this lack of predators have on the animals?**

   It would likely cause the animals to behave differently because they do not have to hunt for food or protect themselves against predators.

Ned Kelly: Black Snake

8. **In *Ned Kelly: Black Snake*, why might the author have opened each chapter with a *'fictionalised recount'*?**
   - ○ it shows Ned Kelly as the terrible villain he was
   - ● to tell the *story* of Ned Kelly as well as the *history* of Ned Kelly
   - ○ there was not enough accurate information available
   - ○ it allows the reader to make their own decisions

   ***To tell the story of Ned Kelly as well as the history of Ned Kelly** is the best answer. The writer is using the fictionalised recounts as a means of giving a true history of Ned Kelly in a story format.*

9. **Which sentence best suggests that *Ned Kelly: Black Snake* reveals more about Ned Kelly than other books about the outlaw?**

    ○ '...supported by archival photographs'

    ● '...offers insight into the life of the outlaw'

    ○ '...recounts Kelly's life from his birth'

    ○ '...quotes from correspondence'

    Offers insight into the life of the outlaw *is the best answer. The word 'insight' can be defined as revealing hidden information. The reviewer states that Black Snake offers insight into the life of the outlaw, meaning more information is revealed about the outlaw.*

10. **'This is not a glorification of a criminal career' – what does this mean?**

    It means that the writer does not portray Ned Kelly's criminal career as something to be admired or glorified.

11. **The *main* purpose of this review is to**

    ○ inform the reader about Ned Kelly's history

    ○ inform the reader about the author, Carole Wilkinson

    ● recommend *Ned Kelly: Black Snake* for reading

    ○ explain that this book is different from other histories of Ned Kelly

    Recommend Black Snake for reading *is the best answer. The review is very positive and clearly shows that the reviewer feels the book is worth reading. While the actual book is about Ned Kelly's history, the review itself does not inform the reader about Ned Kelly's history. Nor does the review give much information about the author apart from the manner in which she has written Black Snake. To explain that this book is different from other histories of Ned Kelly is only a small part of the review and not the main purpose.*

12. **This review is**
    - ○ a criticism
    - ○ an argument
    - ○ a comment
    - ● an analysis

    An analysis *is the correct answer. The review is an examination of Black Snake that provides more than a simple comment on the book. It is not a criticism of the book or the writer, and it is not an argument putting forth a 'stance' or 'case' on an issue.*

Greetings from Luanda, Angola

13. **In the first paragraph, Luanda is portrayed as**
    - ○ a desolate landscape
    - ● a place undergoing development
    - ○ a large, bustling city
    - ○ a drab-grey cement city

    A place undergoing development *is the best answer. The first paragraph is dedicated to describing all the building, landscaping and road works occurring in Luanda.*

14. **Why do you think the third paragraph is written in the form of a story?**
    - ○ so that the writing does not become monotonous
    - ○ to ensure that the reader is concentrating
    - ○ to make the scene more impressive
    - ● to show the reader how the poverty in Luanda affects the writer

To show the reader how the poverty in Luanda affects the writer is the best answer. This paragraph is written just after the writer talks of the poverty in Luanda. It is written this way to highlight the poverty and how it affects the writer.

15. *'...this year there seems to be more trees, decorations and "things to buy" than there were last year.'* **What does this suggest?**
    - ○ Christmas is becoming more popular in Luanda
    - ○ the President's mother likes Christmas trees
    - ● Luanda is becoming more prosperous
    - ○ the writer is beginning to like Luanda

    Luanda is becoming more prosperous is the best answer. Much of the letter is dedicated to describing the progress of Luanda, its development and the greater availability of goods.

16. *'... an election, the first for nearly two decades, has brought some hope.'* **What might they be hoping for?**
    - ● less poverty
    - ○ to leave Luanda
    - ○ more Christmas merchandise
    - ○ more markets

    Less poverty is the best answer. The greater variety of goods for sale and an election are signs of a developing nation. Development can lead to less poverty. The writer gives no indication she wishes to leave Luanda.

17. **Why does the writer change her mind and buy a pineapple?**

    Because the writer realises that the lady has a small child to feed and is pregnant with another child. Selling the fruit is the lady's livelihood. The writer feels compelled to help her.

After the Drought

18. **Who is Edward in the story?**

    Edward is the narrator's baby.

19. **The water is described as '*a fetid wave*'. From reading the story, what word could best be used in place of the word *fetid*?**

    - ○ furious
    - ○ slow
    - ● putrid
    - ○ dripping

    Putrid *is the best answer. In the story, we are told that the water was foul-smelling and contained manure, which smells very unpleasant. Both fetid and putrid mean foul-smelling. Furious, slow and dripping are not appropriate alternatives to 'fetid'.*

20. **Why do you think the sky of the previous four years is described as '*tight*'?**

    - ● it had not rained
    - ○ the sky was stretched
    - ○ the sky was blue
    - ○ the sky was full of rain

    It had not rained *is the best answer. The use of the word 'tight', in this context, is to demonstrate that the sky was unyielding and not giving any rain.*

21. **Why does the narrator say '*Of course I'd seen the sky*'?**

    - ○ to add a comic element to the narrative
    - ○ to induce intrigue in the reader
    - ○ to highlight the sky in the narrative
    - ● to suggest that she had been asked a silly question

To suggest that she had been asked a silly question is the best answer. The purpose of answering her mother's question in this way is to show that her mother had asked a silly question. The narrator tells the reader that the sky had not changed in the previous four years, demonstrating that she believes the question to be redundant.

22. **The valley floor is described as '*moving*'. Was it really moving? Please explain your answer.**

    The valley floor was not really moving; it only appeared to be moving because it was covered in moving flood water.

23. **What common writing technique is the writer using when she describes the roaring of the flood as '*louder, louder, louder...*'?**

    - ○ alliteration
    - ● repetition
    - ○ construction
    - ○ tautology

    Repetition *is the correct answer. Repetition, in writing, is the practice of repeating a word or phrase purposefully for emphasis, which is clearly the writer's intention. Alliteration is using a string of words that all begin with the same letter or sound; construction is building; and a tautology is the repeating of something in different words unnecessarily.*

Ancient fossil reveals how the turtle's shell evolved

24. **What is the main discovery discussed in this article?**
    - ● a half-shelled turtle
    - ○ turtles are more than 220 million years old
    - ○ turtle shells form from bony plates
    - ○ the southern Chinese province of Guizhou

*A **half-shelled turtle** is the correct answer. The main purpose of the article is to inform the reader that the discovery of a half-shelled turtle proves the scientific theory that turtle shells evolved from backbones and ribs and not from bony plates. The province of Guizhou is where the fossils were discovered and not a discovery in itself. The fact that turtles are more than 220 million years old, though this is also new information, is not the main discussion point of the article.*

25. **In which period of history did these turtles exist?**
    - ○ Jurassic
    - ○ Guanling
    - ● Triassic
    - ○ Odontochelys

***Triassic** is the correct answer. This information is clearly stated within the caption accompanying the picture.*

26. **According to the article, how does this discovery alter the study of turtles?**
    - ○ it proves the theory that turtle shells originate from bony plates
    - ○ it suggests that modern turtles do not need their upper shells
    - ● it suggests that the upper shells of modern turtles evolved from the ribs
    - ○ it proves that modern turtles do not need their teeth

***It suggests that the upper shells of modern turtles evolved from the ribs** is the correct answer. We know from reading the article that the discovery of the half-shelled turtle serves to disprove the theory of bony plates. There is not enough information in the article to suggest that modern turtles do not need their upper shells or their teeth.*

27. **From reading the text, what word/s could best be used in place of the word '*hypotheses*' (paragraph 6)?**
    - ○ studies
    - ● theories
    - ○ groups of scientists
    - ○ guesses

    Theories is the best answer within the context of the quote which, in the next sentence, uses both the words 'theory' and 'theorise'.

28. **The main purpose of this article is to**
    - ○ instruct
    - ○ argue
    - ● inform
    - ○ hypothesise

    Inform is the correct answer. The article is an informative piece. It does not instruct the reader in any way, nor can it be considered argumentative because it does not take up a particular stance or viewpoint. Though the article discusses the hypotheses of researchers in the field, it does not offer any of its own hypotheses.

29. **The article describes the discovery of these ancient turtles as the '*missing link*' (paragraph 2). This suggests that**
    - ○ scientists now have all the information they need on turtles
    - ○ there were previously no theories on how the turtle shell evolved
    - ○ this presents an entirely new evolutionary theory
    - ● scientists can now show an evolutionary link between turtles and their shell-less ancestors

Scientists can now show an evolutionary link between turtles and their shell-less ancestors is the correct answer. This information is worded in a different way within the second paragraph: '...being hailed as the long-sought missing link between turtles that have full shells and their shell-less ancestors.'

Daylight Saving Time in Australia and Daylight Saving Time Overseas

30. **Which Australian state does not appear to have opposed Daylight Savings at any time?**

    ○ New South Wales

    ○ Queensland

    ● Tasmania

    ○ Victoria

    ○ Western Australia

    ○ Australian Capital Territory

    Tasmania *is the correct answer. In the article there is no reference to Tasmania having any opposition to Daylight Saving Time. The article clearly states that Tasmania would benefit from Daylight Saving more than the mainland states.*

31. **Using your answer from Question 30, why would this state be less opposed to Daylight Saving Time?**

    At a latitude of 44 degrees, Tasmania is the furthest state away from the equator and would benefit most from Daylight Saving.

32. **What does this article reveal about the practice of Daylight Saving Time?**

    - it has been the subject of much contention
    ○ it is more useful for those states that are closer to the equator
    ○ it is always decided upon by referendum
    ○ it has been routinely adopted in Australia without argument

    ***It has been the subject of much contention** is the correct answer. This is demonstrated throughout the text as it discusses differing opinions of Daylight Saving Time within the Australian states as well as between, and within, overseas countries. Though the text tells us that Daylight Savings has been decided upon via referendum in a couple of instances, there is not enough information in the article to suggest that it is always decided upon by referendum. The remaining answers are completely untrue.*

33. **Daylight Saving Time in the US currently runs from the**

    ○ first Sunday in March to the last Sunday in November
    - first Sunday in April to the last Sunday in October
    ○ last Sunday in March to the last Sunday in September
    ○ last Sunday in April to the first Sunday in October

    ***The first Sunday in April to the last Sunday in October** is the correct answer. This information is clearly stated at the top of the second column in the passage on Daylight Saving Time Overseas.*

34. **In the US, Daylight Saving Time was introduced under 'the Uniform Time Act'. Why is this an inappropriate name for the Act?**

    The name was proven to be inappropriate when not all of the states within the US followed the Uniform Time Act. Therefore, a 'Uniform Time' was never applied within the US.

35. **The text tells us that Queensland was reluctant to take on Daylight Saving Time because it is tropical and therefore would not benefit as much from Daylight Savings.**

    This suggests that

    - ○ the tropics are subject to more temperature fluctuations
    - ○ Queensland is largely a rural state
    - ● tropical places are closer to the equator
    - ○ its workers follow the sun rather than the clock

    ***Tropical places are closer to the equator** is the best answer. Though this information is not expressly stated in the text, we can discern this to be the case through the following: The text tells us that as a tropical state, Queensland would not benefit as much from Daylight Savings. The text also tells us that Tasmania would benefit most from Daylight Saving as it is the furthest state away from the equator. By putting these two pieces of information together, we can guess that tropical places are closer to the equator.*

A Discovery About My Weird Aunt

36. **What was the narrator's primary worry about the trip to his aunt's house?**

    - ○ the animals grazing the paddocks producing methane gas
    - ○ his brother being dragged away from the computer
    - ● not being able to relate to his aunt
    - ○ having to listen to the Seventies Super Stupid Show

    ***Not being able to relate to his aunt** is the best answer. The main focus of the piece is the narrator's journey to his aunt's house and his reluctance to go there because 'She's weird'. The title clearly shows that the narrator's aunt is the focus of the story and there are several revealing references throughout the piece that suggest the narrator had difficulty relating to her. For example: 'I knew* the weirder sister would have nothing to talk about to me'; 'She's weird'; and the narrator's subsequent discovery that they 'would be able to communicate after all.'

37. *'...a very tall, very thin pole with a whirring, purring blade.'* **What is the narrator describing?**

    ○ solar power

    ● a wind turbine

    ○ a ride-on mower

    ○ a flag pole

    A wind turbine *is the correct answer. This paragraph is about the narrator's discovery of green energy devices having been installed at his aunt's house since he had last visited. Therefore, the narrator is clearly not referring to a ride-on mower or a flag pole in this sentence. Out of the remaining answers, the description is better fitted to a wind turbine than solar power.*

38. **'I chose to dream of a cleaner, greener, cooler environment.' In this sentence, what is the narrator revealing about himself?**

    ○ he is tired of listening to music

    ● he is a conservationist

    ○ he does not understand his aunt

    ○ he believes fat and sugar are bad for people

    He is a conservationist *is the correct answer. The sentence clearly indicates that the narrator is an environmentalist. Conservationist is another word for environmentalist. This description does not fit any of the other answers.*

39. **What realisation does the narrator reach?**

    ○ his mother is also a greenie

    ○ his brother does not share his beliefs

    ○ barbeques produce methane gas

    ● his aunt is sympathetic to his cause

    His aunt is sympathetic to his cause *is the best answer. The narrator's discovery about his 'weird aunt' is that his aunt is a fellow environmentalist. She 'had gone green.' This shows that she was sympathetic to the narrator's cause, the environment.*

40. **What is one effect of this story being told in the first person?**

    ○ it gives the impression of distance from the scene

    ● it offers deeper insight into the mindset of the narrator

    ○ it allows the reader to feel compassion toward the other characters

    ○ it enables the writer to comment with a superior approach

    It offers deeper insight into the mindset of the narrator *is the best answer. This piece is clearly written from the narrator's point of view and offers little in the way of compassion for the other characters. A first person approach gives the reader the impression of closeness to the scene as opposed to distance; and a first person approach reveals the intimate thoughts of the narrator, hence offering a deeper insight into the narrator's mindset.*

Wellington

41. **'Those buildings made with glass, steel and brick are laid squat on the key.'** **What does this reveal about buildings of this type in Wellington?**

    ○ they are laid down gently

    ○ they are all flat-roofed

    ● they are not tall high-rises

    ○ they all look the same

    They are not tall high-rises is the best answer. The term 'squat' in this context means short and thickset. A tall high-rise building has many floors and, as the term suggests, rises high up into the sky. There is no indication in the text that the buildings are flat-roofed, that they are laid down gently or that they all look the same, but the term 'squat' does tell us that these buildings are not tall high-rises.

42. **Why do the letterboxes seem 'homeless'?**

    The letterboxes seem homeless because they are up at the side of the road and the houses are tucked down in the hills below.

43. **What does the phrase 'yachts swarming on the bay' imply?**

    ○ the yachts look like ants

    ● there are many yachts sailing in the bay

    ○ the yachts don't know where they are going

    ○ the yachts are moored

    There are many yachts sailing in the bay is the best answer. The word 'swarming' in this context can be construed as a simile for 'abundant' or 'brimming'.

44. **Wellington is described in the text as a '*sea-smacked*' city. What does this suggest?**
    - ● the city's coastal sea can be fierce
    - ○ the city is an island
    - ○ the city's buildings are eroding
    - ○ the city is a naval port

    ***The city's coastal sea can be fierce** is the best answer. The image this phrase evokes is of the sea smacking against the land, which implies fierce or rough sea conditions.*

45. **What word below best describes the style of writing used in this piece?**
    - ○ conversational
    - ○ dictatorial
    - ○ satirical
    - ● descriptive

    ***Descriptive** is the correct answer. The writing is a creative description of Wellington. Stylistically, the writer is not 'conversing' with the reader, nor 'dictating' to the reader and the piece is not a satire.*

46. **'Here, the land folds over itself in wrinkles and bulges.' This phrase is**
    - ○ fictional
    - ○ literal
    - ● metaphorical
    - ○ demonstrative

    ***Metaphorical** is the correct answer. The writer is using a metaphor to convey the many hills and valleys of the land. The land is not literally or actually folding over itself. The piece is a creative description of a real place, making 'fictional' an inappropriate answer. The phrase is not a demonstration.*

Language conventions

Spelling

The spelling mistakes in these sentences have been circled. Write the correct spelling for each circled word in the box.

1. Humans will need to investigate (renewabbel) — renewable

2. sources of energy to (adress) — address

3. the (enourmitty) of the problems — enormity

4. (curantly) faced by the world through global warming. — currently

5. Jack showed his strength when he carried that heavy sack of (potatos) all the way home. — potatoes

6. Everyone comments on how (musculler) — muscular

7. he is, but it was still very (impresive.) — impressive

8. He wore a (disgize) that was so — disguise

9. effective that not even his own family could (gess) who he was.

| guess |

**Each sentence has one word that is incorrect.
Write the correct spelling of the word in the box.**

10. I don't want to make a dental apointment.

| appointment |

11. This is the highest temprature ever recorded.

| temperature |

12. Wendy looked glamerous in her new outfit.

| glamorous |

13. Hippopotamuses can be very feroshus animals.

| ferocious |

14. She studied hard for her quallifications.

| qualifications |

15. Thongs are not apropprate as formal dress.

| appropriate |

16. Bad behaviour should have a consequense.

| consequence |

17. Their going to Europe on a vacation. — They're

18. The detour was a great inconveniance. — inconvenience

19. The car stood motionless in trafic. — traffic

20. Enthusiasm is another word for pasion. — passion

21. Jo feels priviledged to reside in Australia. — privileged

22. His study habits prepared him for the examanation. — examination

23. The origin of the universe is a mistery. — mystery

24. Tran got a sneak preeview of the movie. — preview

25. Mark loves recieving presents on his birthday. — receiving

Grammar and punctuation

26. Which of the following correctly completes the sentence?

Tom _____ better, but he did not want to.

would have done	had done	could have done	done
○	○	●	○

27. Which sentence has the correct punctuation?

● Did he say, "Good morning, Dave"?

○ Did he say "Good morning,Dave"?

○ Did he say good morning Dave?

○ Did he say, "Good morning, Dave?"

28. Which of the following correctly completes the sentence?

I asked, " _____ bag has been left on the floor?"

Whose'	Who's	Whos	Whose
○	○	○	●

29. Which of the following correctly completes the sentence?

She _____ for a long time about her actions before she made that apology.

has thought	had thought	thinks	will think
○	●	○	○

30. Which of the following correctly completes the sentences?

   I'm confused. Raffy said that he would be late, _____ he arrived on time.

so	yet	when	if
○	●	○	○

31. Which of the following correctly completes the sentence?

   They _____ driven more slowly in the rain.

should of	should'ave	should've	shouldve
○	○	●	○

32. Which sentence has the correct punctuation?

   ○ Our societys future will rely upon people's willingness to act.

   ○ Our societies future will rely upon people's willingness to act.

   ○ Our society's future will rely upon peoples willingness to act.

   ● Our society's future will rely upon people's willingness to act.

33. Which of the following correctly completes the sentence?

   He drove the car _____ .

extremely quickly	extreme quick	extreme quickly	extremely quick
●	○	○	○

34. Which of the following correctly completes the sentence?

The restaurant had an _____ atmosphere that attracted customers.

vibrant	warm	alluring	joyful
○	○	●	○

35. Shade one bubble to show where the missing question mark (?) should go.

Did you just ask, "Which questions should I do," even though I just told you
   ○   ○   ○   ●

36. Which sentence has the correct punctuation?

○ Taylor plays the piano; but Sam plays the guitar.

● Taylor plays the piano; Sam plays the guitar.

○ Taylor plays the piano; and Sam plays the guitar.

○ Taylor plays the piano. Sam plays the guitar;

37. Which of the following has the correct punctuation?

● Stephan's mum drove him to school. He doesn't like walking.

○ Stephans mum drove him to school. He doesn't like walking.

○ Stephan's mum drove him to school. He doesnt like walking.

○ Stephan's mum drove him to school he doesn't like walking.

38. Which of the following correctly completes the sentence?

Some people prefer savoury food _____ sweet food.

from	than	to	for
○	○	●	○

39. Which sentence has the correct punctuation?

○ Bring three things a pen, some paper: and something to eat.

○ Bring three things a pen, some paper and something to eat.

○ Bring three things: a pen some paper, and something to eat.

● Bring three things: a pen, some paper and something to eat.

40. Which of the following has the correct punctuation?

○ If you are ill. You should see a doctor.

○ If you are ill; you should see a doctor.

○ If you are ill: you should see a doctor.

● If you are ill, you should see a doctor.

41. Which sentence has the correct punctuation?

○ Suddenly a large bird swooped down swallowed a bug and flew off.

● Suddenly, a large bird swooped down, swallowed a bug and flew off.

○ Suddenly a large bird, swooped down, swallowed a bug, and flew off.

○ Suddenly a large bird swooped down, swallowed a bug and, flew off.

Answers 105

42. Which sentence has the correct punctuation?
    - ○ The book, that I borrowed, from you was, excellent.
    - ○ The book, that I borrowed from you, was excellent.
    - ○ The book that I borrowed from you, was excellent.
    - ● The book that I borrowed from you was excellent.

43. The word *Internet* is capitalised because it is
    - ● a proper noun
    - ○ a common noun
    - ○ an adjective
    - ○ an adverb

44. In the last sentence, the word *links* is used as
    - ○ a proper noun
    - ○ a common noun
    - ● a verb
    - ○ an adverb

45. This text is written in the
    - ● past tense.
    - ○ present tense
    - ○ future tense

46. In the first sentence, the word *Banjo* is in inverted commas (' ') because
    - ○ it is a strange word
    - ● it is a nickname
    - ○ it is a word from a foreign language
    - ○ it is a technical word

47. The word *famous* used before *Waltzing Matilda* is used as
    - ○ a proper noun
    - ● a common noun
    - ● an adjective
    - ○ an adverb
48. This text has been written in the
    - ● first person
    - ○ second person
    - ○ third person
49. '*Our universe is expanding like an inflating balloon*' is an example of
    - ● a simile
    - ○ a metaphor
    - ○ alliteration
    - ○ personification
50. '*Our universe is one big inflating balloon*' is an example of a
    - ○ a simile
    - ● a metaphor
    - ○ alliteration
    - ○ personification

Language conventions answers in detail

Questions 1–25 are spelling mistakes.

Question 26: This question tests modality. The context suggests a need for a modal verb that indicates potential, i.e. *could*.

Question 27: The reported speech is, "Good morning, Dave" and therefore needs to be enclosed within inverted commas, using a capital letter to open. Convention requires a comma before the reported speech begins, and a comma before the name of someone being addressed. The sentence as a whole is a question, so requires a question mark. This comes outside the inverted commas because a question has not been asked within the reported speech, but rather, the reported speech forms part of the question.

Question 28: *Whose* is the standard possessive form of the pronoun *who*.

Question 29: The second clause uses the past tense of *make*, which is *made*, and to have agreement with the first clause, the only option was the past tense of *think*, which from the options was the perfect past form 'had thought'.

Question 30: The sentence requires a coordinating conjunction, and the only one to make sense is 'yet'.

Question 31: The phrase being contracted is 'should have', which is *should've*.

Question 32: The 'future' in the sentence belongs grammatically to the 'society', and the 'willingness to act' belongs grammatically to the 'people', therefore each requires the singular possessive inflection: 's.

Question 33: The appropriate phrase has to feature two adverbs. The first adverb *extremely* is used to modify the adverb *quickly*, which has been used to modify the verb *drove*.

Question 34: The adjective to follow the indefinite article *an* has to begin with a vowel.

Question 35: The question mark comes at the end of the interrogative sentence; the reported question forms only a part of the overall question.

Question 36: The semi-colon is used to separate two clauses not linked by a conjunction. The sentence ends with a full stop.

Question 37: There are two clauses, which require separating with some punctuation (in the examples provided, a full stop). *Mum* belongs to *Stephan*, and so requires a singular possessive inflection: *'s*, and *doesn't* is a contraction requiring an apostrophe to indicate omission.

Question 38: *To* is the only preposition that is appropriate in Standard English usage.

Question 39: A colon is required before the items to be listed, and there needs to be a comma between each element in the list. The sentence needs to end in a full-stop.

Question 40: A comma is required for the fronted clause *if you are ill*.

Question 41: The sentence begins with a capital letter and ends with a full stop. There is a comma after the adverbial *suddenly*, and in the compound sentence, a comma is used to mark off each of the three clauses: *a large bird swooped down* and *swallowed a bug* and *and flew off*.

Question 42: There is no punctuation required in the single clause sentence other than the capital letter to begin and the full stop to end.

Question 43: From the list, only proper nouns are capitalised, and *Internet* is a proper noun.

Question 44: *Links* in the sentence is a verb.

Question 45: The verbs are past tense.

Question 46: The convention is for nicknames to be placed within inverted commas.

Question 47: *Famous* modifies the proper noun *Waltzing Matilda*, so it is an adjective.

Question 48: *We* is first person plural.

Question 49: The universe is being compared to an inflatable balloon, so it is a simile.

Question 50: The universe is described as being the same thing as a one big inflating balloon, so it is a metaphor.

Numeracy non-calculator

1. Each number is 6 less than the number before it. Missing number is 88 − 6 = **82**

2. Isosceles triangle, so the base angles are both 50. Angles in a triangle add to 180. $x = 180 - 100 =$ **80**

3. x values are positive and negative so cannot be the top two graphs. y values are only positive, so **the first graph in the bottom row.**

4. 141, 143, 147, 147, 149, 150 are the only values less than 152, so **6**

5. Opposite sides of a rectangle are equal so $3x - 10 = 2x + 7$ so **x = 17**

6. G:Y $\frac{1}{6} : \frac{5}{6}$ = **1:5**

7. 120 × 1000 m in 60 × 60 secs so

   $\frac{120 \times 1000}{60 \times 60}$ in 1 sec = $\frac{2 \times 1000}{1 \times 60} = \frac{1 \times 1000}{1 \times 30} = \frac{100}{3} = \mathbf{33\frac{1}{3}}$ **m**

8. He needs to go **3 km west and 4 km south**

9. 300 × 0.7 = 30 × 7 = **210**

10. There are 4 green sections out of a total of 8 sections. Chance of green is 4:8 = **1:2**

11. −5(2 − 3x) = **−10 + 15x**

12. a = 100 + 30 = **130**

13. There were two rests as seen by the horizontal lines. One for half an hour and one for an hour giving a total of $\mathbf{1\frac{1}{2}}$ **hours.**

14. 33 ÷ 22 = 1 and remainder 11. $1\frac{11}{22} = \mathbf{1\frac{1}{2}}$

15. X is the base. D comes up as a side and E wraps around to form another side. B comes up as a side and C wraps around to form another side. A folds across as the top. Hence, **A is opposite X.**

16. 360 − 25 = **335°**

17. Area of triangle = $\frac{1}{2} \times b \times h = \frac{1}{2} \times 8 \times 6 =$ **24 cm²**

18. $1.25 + 0.035 =$ **1.285 L**

19. $0.03 \times 100 =$ **3%**

20. $\frac{y}{2} = x + 6$ so $y = 2x + 12$. The only given point that satisfies this is **(2,16)**, since $16 = 2 \times 2 + 12$

21. $8.4 \div 0.4 = 84 \div 4 =$ **21**

22. $\frac{x}{x-5} = 6$, so $x = 6(x-5)$. $x = 6x - 30$. $5x = 30$. **x = 6**

23. Turning to the left for three-quarters of a turn gives the **second shape from the left** in the answers.

24. Jack plays 4. Jill plays 3 other matches not counting her match against Jack which has already been counted. Phil plays 2 other matches and Poppy plays one other match. All of Iris's matches have been counted.

    Total number of matches = $4 + 3 + 2 + 1 =$ **10**

25. $x + (x+1) + (x+2) = 3x + 3 = 174$
    $3x = 171$. $x =$ **57**

26. All the end cubes, i.e. **12**

27. $5 \times (-2)^3 = 5 \times -8 =$ **−40**

28. The graph $y = 3x$ passes through the origin, so not the two graphs on the left-hand side. It has a positive gradient, so the answer is **the second graph in the top row**.

29. $10 \times 10 \times 10 =$ **1,000**

30. Bev sets out with $\frac{3}{4} \times \frac{72}{1} = 54$ L. She uses 27 L and has 27 L left. To fill tank needs $72 - 27 =$ **45 L**

31. At second stop $\frac{1}{4} \times \frac{2}{3} = \frac{1}{6}$ get off.
   Fraction off at first and second stops $= \frac{1}{3} + \frac{1}{6} = \frac{1}{2}$
   At third stop $\frac{1}{2} \times \frac{1}{2} = \frac{1}{4}$ get off. Fraction off at all three stops $= \frac{1}{2} + \frac{1}{4} = \frac{3}{4}$.
   Fraction remaining $= \frac{1}{4} = 6$, so $\frac{4}{4} = 24$

32. $x = 90 + 60 = \mathbf{150°}$

Numeracy calcluator

1. **First answer on the left**
2. $\left(5\frac{2}{3} + 8\frac{1}{3}\right) \div 2 = \mathbf{7}$
3. $(11.7 + 14.42 + 16.84) \div 3 = \mathbf{14.32}$
4. $3 \times 9 = \mathbf{27}$
5. **The dotted line on the picture on the right.**
6. Beth took the same time to walk a greater distance than Amy, so **Beth walked faster than Amy.**
7. **B**
8. $A = \pi \times r^2 = \pi \times 0.7^2 = \mathbf{2}$
9. $\dfrac{10 \times 4}{5 \times 4 - 10} = \dfrac{40}{10} = \mathbf{4}$
10. Check the alternatives to see if the x values give the corresponding y values. $\mathbf{y = (x - 3)^2}$
11. There are 20 unshaded squares. Grouping these in fours gives 5 groups each with an area of 25. Total area = $5 \times 25 = \mathbf{125\ m^2}$
12. 40% not in choir. 40% = 156, 10% = 39, 100% = **390**
13. $3m + 3 + m - 21 = 90$
    $4m = 108$
    $\mathbf{m = 27}$
14. $\dfrac{1}{2} \times 16 \times h = 160$
    $h = 20$
    New height = 10, new base = 8
    New area = $\dfrac{1}{2} \times 8 \times 10 = \mathbf{40\ cm^2}$
15. C(for small circle) $= \pi \times D = 6.4\pi$ C(for large circle) $= \pi \times D = 25.6\pi$
    Ratio: $6.4\pi : 25.6\pi = \mathbf{1:4}$

Answers

16. $y = 25 - 5 \times 3.15 = \mathbf{9.25}$

17. 4:20 pm till 4:20 am is 12 hours. There are another 3 hours till 7:20 am, i.e. 15 hours. Trip finished at 7:14 am, i.e. 6 minutes less, so **14 hours 54 minutes**

18. Length $= 115 \div 6.25 = \mathbf{18.4 \text{ m}}$

19. Base angle of isosceles triangle $= 65$. $65 + a = 90$, $\boldsymbol{a = 25}$

20. This year's increase $= \dfrac{30}{100} \times \dfrac{280}{1} = 84$

    This year she gets $280 + 84 = 364$

    Next year's increase $= \dfrac{20}{100} \times \dfrac{364}{1} = 72.80$

    Next year she gets $364 + 72.80 = \mathbf{\$436.80}$

21. **436.26**

22. $30\% = 42$

    $1\% = \dfrac{42}{30}$

    $100\% = \dfrac{42}{30} \times 100 = \mathbf{140}$

23. Unmarked angle $= 180 - (89 + 15) = 76$.

    $a = 180 - (76 + 32) = \mathbf{72}$.

24. $C = an + b$

    $22.20 = 12a + b$ \quad (1)

    $39 = 60a + b$ \quad (2)

    $(2) - (1) \rightarrow 16.8 = 48a \rightarrow a = 0.35$

    Substitute in $(2) \rightarrow 39 = 21 + b \rightarrow b = 18$

    $\mathbf{18 + 0.35n}$

25. $\dfrac{1}{2} \times 9.8 \times 3^2 = \mathbf{44.1 \text{ m}}$

26. $\dfrac{x}{0.4} = \dfrac{48}{0.32}$

   $x = \dfrac{48}{0.32} \times 0.4 =$ **60 m**

27. Number of people surveyed = 6 + 18 + 10 + 4 + 2 = **40**

28. 63 × 5 − 2 = **313**

29. **$2p^2 + 5$**

30. $(x + 2) \times (x - 7) =$ **$x^2 - 5x - 14$**

31. Youngest gets $x

    Middle child gets $2x

    Eldest gets $4x

    $4x + 2x + x = 7x = 245$, so $x =$ **$35**

32. Total height of all students = 152 × 24 = 3,648

    Total height when Suzie joins class = 3,648 + 127 = 3,775

    Average height = 3,775 ÷ 25 = **151 cm**

www.ingramcontent.com/pod-product-compliance
Ingram Content Group UK Ltd.
Pitfield, Milton Keynes, MK11 3LW, UK
UKHW021408070725
6762UKWH00032B/1014